Blood's been spilled to afford us this moment . . . *now*.
See what it is before you. See the here and now. That's the
hardest thing, the only thing that accounts. Abolishing
slavery by constitutional provision settles the fate, for all
coming time, not only of the millions now in bondage but
of unborn millions to come.

✦ ✦ ✦

President Abraham Lincoln addressing his cabinet
From *Lincoln*, written by Tony Kushner

A STEVEN SPIELBERG FILM

LINCOLN

A CINEMATIC AND HISTORICAL COMPANION

Forewords by
Steven Spielberg & Kathleen Kennedy

Afterword by Tony Kushner

Text by David Rubel

Interviews for *Filming Lincoln*
by Laurent Bouzereau

Design by H. Clark Wakabayashi

A WELCOME BOOK

NEW YORK

CONTENTS

· · ·

FOREWORD

✦ ✦ ✦

STEVEN SPIELBERG

IN ITS OPENING LINES, our Declaration of Independence optimistically asserts that God created people with the right to live, to be free, and to pursue happiness. American democracy, as first expressed in the Declaration and as established in our Constitution, is meant to be optimistic; it was designed to be a rational system that ensures justice, liberty, and perhaps even progress through a balanced division of the powers of the state, through civil discourse and compromise, and through a dynamic yet stable relationship between the people and our local, state, and national governments—and a good deal of the time, it mostly works! We Americans are justifiably proud of the reasonableness and reliability of our machinery of government, which has produced in us a generally positive, can-do spirit. Given all of this sunny, unshadowed expectation, it's surprising how central to our national experience tragedy has been. There's a lot of bloodshed behind American progress.

Perhaps this is true of all human progress, for the history of our species has been bloody as often as it's been life-affirming, savage as often as it's been civilized, cruel as often as it's been kind. But the men and women who created our country envisioned it as a step forward, out of the darkness of tyranny and war, and into some new, enlightened way in which people can live together without destroying one another, and so the gore in which American history is steeped seems an affront to those luminous ideals.

Americans for the most part are as aware of our legacy of violence as we are of our heritage of reason, and we regard this as a paradox, rather than as hypocrisy. Our political leaders tell us we are a decent, generous, and peaceable people, and they aren't wrong. But the news tells us every day that our society is haunted by and saturated with old hatreds, irrational prejudices, and scapegoats old and new; we liberate ourselves from our social demons almost always after a great spasm of rage in which lives are lost.

In the twentieth century, my peers and I watched or participated in a national rejection of the evils of racial segregation and the first attempts to create, at very long last, a society truly dedicated to the realization of human equality and dignity regardless of race. Much progress has been made in this regard, slower than would have been ideal but faster than many of us would have anticipated. American democracy and the due process of law helped create these transformations. But no one can understand the triumphs of the African American civil rights movement without considering the one hundred years of Jim Crow segregation and lynching that preceded them. No one can entirely separate the movement's most glorious, inspiring moments, such as the Selma march or Martin Luther King Jr. speaking at the Lincoln Memorial, from the horror of four little girls being blown up in a church, or the three young men murdered in Mississippi. The beauty of the memory of Dr. King is indelibly stained with his martyr's blood. As civil rights workers know, just as the soldiers on Omaha Beach on D-Day knew, democracy offers promises of reason, justice, happiness, liberty, and peace, but often terrible sacrifice is required before these promises can be realized.

It's a fascinating aspect of human nature that we have the capacity—and perhaps, alarmingly, even the need—to learn from tragedy. We look for explanations, analyses of broad historical forces, but these seem impersonal, beyond the control of most of us. We turn from the impersonal to the personal, to examples of people who managed not only to survive tragedy but also to emerge with their humanity intact. We seek the example of those who refuse to follow the destructive courses we sometimes venture upon. We fasten attention on those among us who manage to emerge from the fire or rise from the ashes with a vision of a healed and better world, those who find not bitterness in tragedy, but hope, those who can lead us forward. We read our history to discover such people, and we watch the news to find them in our midst.

I suppose this can be called hero worship, and I know that in a democracy, such worship has its serious dangers. The people, after all, and not the people's heroes, keep democracy alive. But isn't there a difference between the kind of worship—idolatry, really—that comes from a desire to be saved, and the kind of admiration that comes from a need to learn, a need to assume rather than abdicate responsibility?

When exploring the four exceedingly bloody and hard years of the Civil War, it's impossible not to see Abraham Lincoln as our very own phoenix, emerging from unimaginable devastation to insist that we can be better than we have been, to show us that it's possible to transform the bloodiest war in American history into a means, even if a tragic means, by which a great proposition, that all are created equal, has been tested and found true. If we regard Lincoln this way, are we worshipping him, or do we simply hope to learn from him? We seem always to have wanted to get close to him, not to idolize but to understand him, to be uplifted and galvanized by this man, this pragmatist, this realist, this openhearted and, at times, suffering man who was a steadfast optimist in the name of freedom and equality.

I arrived to begin shooting in Richmond, Virginia, afraid that audiences for this film would only ever see the iconic, immobile face seared into our brains from Mount Rushmore or from the American penny. But I knew the minute I showed up, my first day on the set, that we were a group of people for whom Lincoln is a vital, urgent presence, not only in history but in the present moment. It was as if Daniel Day-Lewis, his fellow cast members, and all of us on the crew had made a silent and solemn promise: to strive to honor not only the memory of Lincoln, and the past in which he worked and struggled, but also to honor the way in which Lincoln continues to speak, to insist, to urge us forward into a future worthy of America's most beautiful ideals.

Doris Kearns Goodwin's masterpiece of synthesis and historical narrative, *Team of Rivals*, was the source and guiding spirit for Tony Kushner's script, examining Lincoln as a man, a husband and father, and president and political tactician of peerless skill during his battle to establish a permanent and legal basis for abolishing slavery. Daniel seems to have been born to play Abraham Lincoln. Beyond the remarkable physical resemblance that made our work infinitely easier, and beyond Daniel's immense, legendary talent, plus his artistic acuity and extraordinary ear for the rhythms of speech, he brought to the work a courage, commitment, toughness, gentleness, generosity, and discipline that left everyone who worked on the film, including its director, feeling grateful, a little awestruck, and eager to follow. We worked very hard, and I'm indebted to everyone on the film, behind and in front of the camera, who came together to shape this story.

When his secretary of war, Edwin Stanton, said at the president's deathbed that Lincoln would "belong to the ages," he was, it turns out, simply speaking the truth. Lincoln's murder was a catastrophe for the country, for the human race. And yet, as Lincoln has shown us by example, death can also be a portal, not into Heaven, but into the future life of the world.

FOREWORD

❖ ❖ ❖

KATHLEEN KENNEDY

THAT OUR LIVES might be written for us is a fundamental, philosophical debate that we struggle to reconcile our entire lives. What is our purpose? And how might we come to realize it? For the precious few, those who time so rarely grants the human race and who are completely fitted to their place and period, we know that an answer is attainable. What we so often fail to realize, however, is the cost of that personal prescience, for those whose true destiny is revealed to them.

"Do you think we choose to be born? Are we fitted to the time we're born into?"

The words above—although written by Tony Kushner, spoken by Daniel Day-Lewis, and directed by Steven Spielberg—could have easily been uttered by our sixteenth president, in his own search for an answer. Abraham Lincoln was elected to the highest seat of political power as the United States was headed over the precipice, into the darkest period of our history. He accepted his position willingly, and with perfect clarity of purpose: the nation must be preserved. Despite and in spite of constantly changing tides, his presidency never lost sight of that principal principle. The enormity of the burden that comes with such responsibility is inconceivable, when we consider the lives that were lost to preserve the Union, end slavery, keep alive the delicate flame of democracy, and begin to heal a deeply wounded country. It is difficult to imagine that someone would rise to that challenge; it is even most difficult to imagine the kind of person that would rise so wholly, so selflessly, and with unconditional dedication.

While I will never truly know him, the experience of making this film was still a very intimate process of discovery. Many of us who had the honor to be a part of such a production immersed ourselves in the world of Abraham Lincoln and who he was as a person: caring, vulnerable, steadfast, lonely, powerful, intelligent, and wickedly funny. As we peeled back the layers of his character through volumes of firsthand accounts and one hundred and fifty years of historical interpretation, many of my personal

preconceptions of "Honest Abe" were shaken to their core. The Lincoln I learned of in school, the legend of which I'm reminded every time I spend a penny, drive down a street or through a town bearing his name, or hear his politics invoked on Capitol Hill, was more complex a man, more layered, and vastly more complicated than what I could have ever envisioned.

On one hand, Lincoln possessed an enduring spirit and unwavering optimism in humanity; on the other, he was a man shaped by extreme tragedy and bitter loss. With the death of his own son from illness, he understood the consequence of civil war and the toll it would take on the families who lost their own loved ones. Beyond the suffering caused by the conflict, he saw the good in a country that lay nearly in ruins, and recognized reason to save it. This defiance was also tempered by compassion; he would spend hours meeting with members of the public in his own office, personally handling the largest problem to the smallest. He would solicit advice from the politically diametric members of his cabinet before coming to a decision, and then, when a decision was made, he would stand by it. He came from humble beginnings, and remained humble without ever allowing his past to keep him from meeting his potential. And although so many opposed him, he rallied countless more to his cause.

Accurately depicting the many nuances of such an iconic figure came with many challenges; the initial difficulty was identifying that pivotal time in Lincoln's life that would epitomize his politics, his personal life, and the obstacles that stood in his way. In addition to the information provided by Doris Kearns Goodwin's book, Tony Kushner did extensive investigation of his own before putting every detail of Lincoln's life during the period of the film down on paper. Steven Spielberg distilled those ideas down to the essential moments that would define Lincoln's legacy.

Lincoln's accomplishments will forever secure his place in history, but it is his character that brings so many back to him, time and again, for a deeper look. Revealing the essence of Lincoln was perhaps the biggest challenge of all; Daniel Day-Lewis, one of the best actors of our time, not only physically captures Lincoln's stature and profound charisma, but he manages to also transport us in time back to the events that so shaped our nation into what it is today. Daniel Day-Lewis as Lincoln gives us the image that helps to remind and reinforce the memory of such a remarkable individual, whose impact has touched generations, and will continue to touch many generations yet to come. ꧁

PART ONE

PLAYERS ON THE STAGE OF HISTORY

I have an irrepressible desire to live till I can be assured that

the world is a little better for my having lived in it.

—ABRAHAM LINCOLN

ABRAHAM LINCOLN

President of the United States

❖ ❖ ❖

PORTRAYED BY DANIEL DAY-LEWIS

THE Abraham Lincoln familiar to contemporary Americans is literally larger than life. But the face we know from the Lincoln Memorial and Mount Rushmore is the visage of the iconic Lincoln, not the mug of the dark-horse frontier lawyer who surprisingly became president.

The Lincoln that most Americans knew in 1860, when six out of ten people voted for someone else, was an unattractive, somewhat vulgar bumpkin who seemed overmatched by the crisis at hand. Remembered now for the beauty and insight of his speeches, Lincoln has benefited from the lack of recording technology. Although one is tempted to infer a cultivated speaking voice to match the sophistication of the words, Lincoln actually spoke in a high-pitched voice with a strong frontier accent.

In manner as well, Lincoln was unabashedly a commoner. "When at rest or listening, his legs and arms seemed to hang almost lifeless, and his face was care-worn and haggard," Maj. Gen. William T. Sherman wrote; "but, the moment he began to talk, his face lightened up, his tall form, as it were, unfolded, and he was the very impersonation of good-humor and fellowship."

On the other hand, Lincoln's modesty and humility were not entirely authentic. "The man who thinks Lincoln calmly sat down and gathered his robes about him, waiting for the people to call him, has a very erroneous knowledge of Lincoln," his law partner William H. Herndon wrote. "He was always calculating, and always planning ahead. His ambition was a little engine that knew no rest."

After meeting Lincoln in March 1865, Col. Theodore Lyman, a wealthy Harvard graduate and urbane world traveler, wrote this assessment for his wife: "The President is, I think, the ugliest man I ever put my eyes on; there is also an expression of plebeian vulgarity in his face that is offensive (you recognize the recounter of coarse stories). On the other hand, he has the look of sense and wonderful shrewdness, while the heavy eyelids give him a mark almost of genius. He strikes me, too, as a very honest and kindly man; and, with all his vulgarity, I see no trace of low passions in his face. On the whole, he is such a mixture of all sorts, as only America brings forth. . . . I never wish to see him again, but, as humanity runs, I am well content to have him at the head of affairs."

MARY TODD LINCOLN

First Lady of the United States

— ◆ ◆ ◆ —

PORTRAYED BY SALLY FIELD

MARY Todd Lincoln was probably the most controversial first lady in American history. Although cheerful and cordial much of the time, she was prone to fits of abusive temper and other erratic behavior that persuaded most Washingtonians to keep their distance. Historians have since speculated that she suffered from bipolar disorder; but that diagnosis didn't exist at the time, and most people simply considered her, in the words of presidential secretary John Hay, "a hellcat."

Some of the rancor can no doubt be attributed to social rivalry. But even those wishing to like Mary—such as Lt. Comdr. John S. Barnes, who accompanied her to City Point in March 1865—found the first lady so difficult that she strained Victorian courtesy. "She was at no time well," Barnes wrote; "the mental strain upon her was great, betrayed by extreme nervousness approaching hysteria, causing misapprehensions, [and] extreme sensitiveness as to slights or want of politeness or consideration. I had the greatest sympathy for her, and for Mr. Lincoln, who I am sure felt deep anxiety for her."

Born and raised in Lexington, Kentucky, an up-and-coming town that her family had helped to found, Mary suffered a deep emotional blow at six years of age when her mother died in childbirth. But she adored her father, and that attachment sustained her. A wealthy and influential slaveholder, Robert Todd entertained many great men of the day and enjoyed showing off his bright, vivacious daughter. Basking in the approbation, Mary developed a lifelong interest in politics—which to her meant parties and personalities, not strategies and issues.

In 1839, the twenty-one-year-old Mary joined her married sister Elizabeth Todd Edwards in Springfield, Illinois. Family lore has it that Mary once declared she would marry a future president, and her suitors in Springfield included four future U.S. senators (Stephen Douglas among them), but she chose the awkward country lawyer Abraham Lincoln. Whatever Lincoln's ambitions may have been at the time, his new wife certainly urged him on to loftier ones.

After the death of her eleven-year-old son Willie in February 1862, Mary's mental state collapsed, and she entered a depression so deep and prolonged that her husband feared she would drive herself mad. That never occurred, but her behavior never truly stabilized, and her reputation never improved. After her husband's martyrdom, it took a reluctant Congress five years to grant the impoverished widow a pension.

ROBERT LINCOLN

Eldest Son of the President

❖ ❖ ❖

PORTRAYED BY JOSEPH GORDON-LEVITT

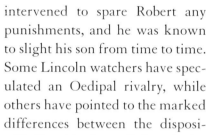

THE Lincolns' first child—named after Mary's father, Robert Todd—was born in August 1843. During much of Robert's childhood, Abraham was away from home, riding Illinois' Eighth Judicial Circuit. His principal memory from those years was of his father packing saddlebags for yet another semiannual trip.

Left for months at a time in the care of his overanxious mother, Robert learned to distance himself from parental authority. A next-door neighbor described Mary Lincoln as "prone to excitability and rather impulsive, saying many things that were sharp and caustic, and which she afterwards usually regretted." She whipped the boy often, sometimes for offenses so slight as falling into a mud puddle.

By 1853, when the last of the Lincoln boys was born, the local railroad network had become developed enough for Abraham to return home on weekends and still maintain a full caseload. As a result, he developed much closer relationships with his younger sons, whom he treated with extreme leniency. "It is my pleasure that my children are free, happy, and unrestrained by parental tyranny," he said.

But this attitude didn't extend to his oldest son, with whom his relationship remained distant. Abraham rarely intervened to spare Robert any punishments, and he was known to slight his son from time to time. Some Lincoln watchers have speculated an Oedipal rivalry, while others have pointed to the marked differences between the dispositions of father and son. Unlike Abraham, Robert had a limited sense of humor, an impulsive nature, an overly strong sense of decorum, and a hankering for wealth along with the gracious living it supported. "He is a Todd and not a Lincoln," Lincoln law partner William H. Herndon concluded.

In 1859, when Robert was sixteen, his parents sent him away to Phillips Exeter Academy in New Hampshire. A year later, he entered Harvard College. During school holidays, he visited his family at the White House. Washington society welcomed him—appreciating his good looks, excellent manners, and fashionable attire—but he felt stiff and awkward around his father, and both were relieved each time he returned to Cambridge.

"In all my plans for the future," Robert wrote to a professor twelve days after the assassination, "the chief object I had in view was the approbation of my Father, and now that he is gone and in such a way, I feel utterly without spirit or courage."

TAD LINCOLN

Youngest Son of the President

◆ ◆ ◆

PORTRAYED BY GULLIVER McGRATH

THE Lincolns' fourth son, Thomas, was born in April 1853. As a baby, he was "as wiggly as a tadpole," his father said, so the family nicknamed him Tad.

Born with a cleft palate, Tad had a speech impediment that made his words nearly unintelligible to outsiders. The condition worsened when his teeth grew in crookedly, adding a bad lisp; but he nonetheless grew into a rambunctious, spirited child with an impulsive temperament not unlike his mother's.

In Springfield, Tad and his older brother Willie were labeled "hellions" because of their notorious lack of discipline. Abraham Lincoln's partner William H. Herndon wrote of how the boys would pull books off the shelves and otherwise mangle the law office while their father continued to work, apparently oblivious to their behavior. After the family's move to Washington, the White House became their new playground.

In February 1862, Willie and Tad both contracted typhoid fever. Tad recovered, but Willie passed away on February 20 at the age of eleven. After Willie's death, the president became even more devoted to and indulgent of his youngest son. Although the nine-year-old Tad could neither read nor write, for example,

his father refused to compel him to study. "Let him run," Lincoln said. "There's time enough yet for him to learn his letters and get pokey."

"He was as shrewd as he was lawless, and always knew whether he could make a tutor serviceable or not," presidential private secretary John Hay wrote. "If he found one with obstinate ideas of the superiority of grammar to kite-flying as an intellectual employment, he soon found means of getting rid of him."

Tad also frustrated the members of Lincoln's cabinet, frequently interrupting their meetings with the president to demand the attention of Papa Day (his vocalization of "Papa Dear"). Always Lincoln halted the meeting until Tad's needs were met.

Although Hay called the child "the absolute tyrant of the Executive Mansion," he also realized that Lincoln drew unmatched comfort from his young son's ebullience, enjoying few things more than helping Tad play with his toys. Retiring at the end of a long day, Lincoln often found Tad asleep on one of the chairs or couches in his outer office. Picking him up, the president usually carried the boy off to his own bed—where, after Willie's death, Tad mostly slept.

JOHN NICOLAY

Private Secretary to the President

* * *

PORTRAYED BY JEREMY STRONG

JOHN George Nicolay, born in Bavaria in 1832, emigrated to the United States with his family in 1838. After settling in Pike County, Illinois, the sixteen-year-old Nicolay became a printer's devil with the *Pittsfield Free Press*, a Whig newspaper in the county seat. In 1854, now the editor-owner, Nicolay aligned the newspaper with the new Republican party, supporting its successful gubernatorial candidate in 1856. After the election, Nicolay sold the newspaper and moved to Springfield, where he took a job with the office of the Illinois secretary of state, managing its election records.

Because Abraham Lincoln often visited Nicolay's office on political business, the two men became quite well acquainted. Recognizing Nicolay's impressive clerical skills and his methodical, self-effacing personality, Lincoln asked the twenty-eight-year-old to become his private secretary following his nomination for president in May 1860.

Nicolay's primary duty during the 1860 campaign was to manage the candidate's correspondence. He read and sorted the letters that arrived each day, ignoring the ones from lunatics and cranks and replying himself to those a generic response would satisfy. After the election, however, as the daily letter volume increased from forty or fifty to seventy or eighty, Nicolay persuaded Lincoln to hire an assistant secretary, recommending his friend John Hay. Meanwhile, Nicolay became the president-elect's one-man transition team.

At the White House, in addition to managing Lincoln's correspondence, Nicolay screened visitors, prepared news digests, acted as an emissary, and more. During 1864, Nicolay even oversaw the president's reelection campaign.

In carrying out these demanding duties, Nicolay's brusque, Germanic nature served him well. "People who do not like him—because they cannot use him, perhaps—say he is sour and crusty, and it is a grand good thing, then, that he is," White House clerk William O. Stoddard wrote of his superior. "If you will sit in that chair a month or so, you will see what has become of any easy good-nature you sat down with. Hot-tempered fellows like you and me have no business in that chair. . . . The President showed his good judgment of men when he put Mr. Nicolay just where he is."

JOHN HAY

Assistant Private Secretary to the President

PORTRAYED BY JOSEPH CROSS

JOHN Hay first met John Nicolay in 1851, when both were attending the Thompson Academy in Pittsfield, Illinois. Hay was just thirteen years old at the time, but the six years between them didn't prevent their becoming close friends. A year later, Hay entered the Illinois state college in Springfield, from which he transferred to Brown University in 1855. After completing his studies at Brown, Hay returned reluctantly to the frontier and in March 1859 moved back to Springfield to clerk for his uncle Milton, an attorney whose law office adjoined Abraham Lincoln's. Thus, when Nicolay recommended Hay for the post of assistant private secretary, Lincoln already knew the twenty-two-year-old.

At the White House, Nicolay and Hay had separate offices off the main waiting room, but they shared a bedroom that was also part of the second-floor suite. This arrangement made them available to the president, who slept just down the hall, twenty-four hours a day. It also promoted close relationships among the three men. For instance, the president appeared late one night in the secretaries' bedroom, waking them with his laughter. He had been reading an amusing poem, Hay noted in his diary, "seemingly utterly unconscious that he with his short shirt hanging above his long legs and setting out behind like the tail feathers of an enormous ostrich was infinitely funnier than anything in the book he was laughing at."

Both Nicolay and Hay revered Lincoln, and the president returned their devotion, but his relationship with Hay went further. Showing respect for Nicolay, Lincoln always addressed him by his surname; Hay, however, he called "John." According to journalist Noah Brooks, "Lincoln treated Hay with the affection of a father, only with more than a father's freedom. If he waked at night he roused Hay, and they read together; in summer they rode in the afternoons and dined in the evenings at the Soldiers' Home."

As a counterpoint to the somber Nicolay, Hay played the court jester, repeating jokes and enlivening the often-grim mood with his youthful exuberance. The cheerfulness and conviviality with which he greeted visitors appealed to most; but Hay's seemingly unlimited self-confidence irked others, including the first lady, who read him as arrogant. Hay returned the dislike, as did Nicolay—which shouldn't be surprising given that both of them competed with her for the president's attention and affection.

ELIZABETH KECKLEY

Modiste and Confidante to the First Lady

❦ ❦ ❦

PORTRAYED BY GLORIA REUBEN

ELIZABETH Hobbs Keckley was born a slave about 1818. Among her peers, she was considered privileged because she was taught how to read and write at a time when educating slaves was illegal in most Southern states.

Keckley's mother, Agnes, was a house slave owned by Armistead Burwell, a not-so-prosperous planter in Dinwiddie County, Virginia. Although the light-skinned Keckley didn't learn the identity of her father until many years later, she knew even as a girl that he must have been white. Not until Agnes lay dying did she reveal to her daughter that Burwell was both master and father.

When the eldest Burwell son, Robert, married Margaret Robertson in 1832, Keckley was sent to keep house for the newlyweds in Hillsborough, North Carolina. According to Keckley, her new mistress "seemed to be desirous to wreak vengeance on me for something" and asked a neighbor, William Bingham, to beat her until she gave up what he called her "stubborn pride." The project failed. After several whippings, "my suffering at last subdued his hard heart," Keckley wrote. "He asked my forgiveness, and afterwards was an altered man."

Keckley was also abused in Hillsborough by a man named Alexander Kirkland, who forced a sexual relationship on her. After becoming pregnant and giving birth to a son in 1839, Keckley was returned to Virginia, where she joined the family of Ann Burwell Garland. Life with the cash-strapped Garlands was unstable, however, and they rarely stayed in one place very long. Not until 1847 did they settle in St. Louis, where Keckley worked as a seamstress to support the household of seventeen.

Out of economic necessity, Keckley developed close relationships with wealthy white women who appreciated not only her skill as a dressmaker but also her engaging personality. When she finally persuaded her master to set her and her son free for a payment of twelve hundred dollars, it was these women who loaned her the money.

After gaining her freedom in November 1855, Keckley remained in St. Louis until she repaid her debt. Then, in 1860, she moved east, settling in Washington, where her proficiency as a dressmaker attracted the attention of socially prominent women, including Mrs. Jefferson Davis and Mrs. Robert E. Lee. Through one of these women, she was introduced to the new first lady, Mary Todd Lincoln, soon becoming her personal modiste.

WILLIAM H. SEWARD

Secretary of State

— ◆ ◆ ◆ —

PORTRAYED BY DAVID STRATHAIRN

WILLIAM H. Seward and Abraham Lincoln met for the first time on September 22, 1848. The occasion was a large Whig rally at the Tremont Temple in Boston. Both men were touring New England, campaigning for Whig presidential nominee Zachary Taylor. Seward, the former governor of New York, was the featured speaker, known nationally for his uncompromising opposition to slavery.

Like Lincoln, Seward was a rather odd looking fellow. According to Henry Adams, he had a "slouching, slender figure; a head like a wise macaw; a beaked nose; shaggy eyebrows; unorderly hair and clothes; hoarse voice; offhand manner; . . . and [a] perpetual cigar." In the opinion of journalist Noah Brooks, Seward was "affable and pleasant, accessible—from a newspaper point of view—smoking cigars always, ruffled or excited never, astute, keen to perceive a joke, appreciative of a good thing, and fond of 'good victuals.'" He was also rather vain and self-important.

At the rally, Seward spoke first, delivering a lengthy oration that focused not on the usual Whig economic nostrums (internal improvements and protectionist tariffs) but on the need to oppose slavery's expansion into the territories recently taken from Mexico. Lincoln, then a congressman from Illinois, was impressed—realizing, perhaps for the first time, the depth of feeling among some Northerners that slavery and freedom were irreconcilable.

The next day, when both men found themselves in nearby Worcester, they agreed to share a bed for the night—a common practice in mid-nineteenth century hotels. "We spent the greater part of the night talking, I insisting that the time had come for sharp definitions of opinion and boldness of utterance," Seward recalled. "I have been thinking about what you said in your speech," Lincoln admitted. "I reckon you are right. We have got to deal with this slavery question and got to give more attention to it hereafter than we have been doing."

Five months later, the forty-seven-year-old Seward won election to the Senate, where he took part in the historic debates over the Compromise of 1850. In a famous speech delivered on March 11 of that year on the floor of the Senate, Seward asserted that "The Constitution devotes the national domain to union, to justice, to defense, to welfare, and to liberty. But there is a higher law than the Constitution, which regulates our authority over the domain, and devotes it to the same noble purposes."

EDWIN M. STANTON

Secretary of War

◆ ◆ ◆

PORTRAYED BY BRUCE MCGILL

EDWIN McMasters Stanton was an easy man to dislike. He was arrogant, opinionated, quick-tempered, and condescending. He was also highly successful. As one of the most prominent lawyers in the country, he earned fifty thousand dollars a year during the late 1850s, or twice as much as the president.

Abraham Lincoln's first impression of Stanton was nothing if not memorable. In 1855, Lincoln had been retained as local counsel in a major patent case scheduled to be tried in Illinois. Soon thereafter, the venue shifted to Cincinnati, making Lincoln's participation superfluous; but he traveled east nonetheless to deliver his brief. Meanwhile, lead attorney George Harding of Philadelphia engaged Stanton as his local counsel in Ohio.

When Lincoln arrived in Cincinnati, Stanton took one look at his ill-fitting, unfashionable clothes and immediately turned to Harding. "Why did you bring that damned long-armed ape here?" Stanton barked. "He does not know anything and can do you no good." Humiliated, Lincoln withdrew, while Stanton parlayed victory in the case into an even more lucrative legal practice in Washington (where he moved in 1856).

Yet Lincoln was not one to hold grudges, especially when something could be gained from forgiveness. Consequently, when Secretary of War Simon Cameron's incompetence and corruption necessitated his dismissal in January 1862, Lincoln heeded William Seward's advice that he appoint Stanton.

Never lacking in self-confidence, Stanton frequently angered colleagues with rude or insulting behavior and rarely respected their views. On one occasion, he berated Judge Advocate General Joseph Holt for ordering the release of a family of smugglers from prison. When Holt protested that the release had been ordered by the president, Stanton exclaimed, "Well, all I have to say is, we've got to get rid of that baboon at the White House!" When Stanton's insult was repeated to him, the president replied, "Insult? Insult? That is no insult; it is an expression of opinion; and what troubles me most about it is that Stanton said it, and Stanton is usually right."

Lincoln tolerated Stanton's behavior because, as an administrator, he was skillful, energetic, and wholeheartedly devoted to preserving the Union. "Night after night he remained in his office until a late hour and sometimes until daylight," Interior Secretary John P. Usher wrote of Stanton; "not infrequently would his carriage be found standing at the door waiting for him when daylight came."

FRANCIS PRESTON BLAIR, SR.

Cofounder of the Republican Party

❖ ❖ ❖

PORTRAYED BY HAL HOLBROOK

THOUGH born in Virginia, Francis Preston Blair, Sr., grew up in Frankfort, Kentucky, where his father served as state attorney general for twenty-three years and where he became a newspaper editor. During the presidential campaign of 1828, Blair strongly supported the candidacy of Democratic nominee Andrew Jackson. After the election, Blair's continuing pro-administration editorials caught the attention of Old Hickory at a time when he was looking for a skilled, sympathetic voice to take over the *Washington Globe*, the capital's principal Democratic organ. At Jackson's invitation, Blair moved east in 1830, becoming editor of the *Globe* and a member of the president's innermost circle, known as the Kitchen Cabinet.

Blair's impressive rise reached a peak of sorts in 1836, when he purchased a two-story brick mansion at 1651 Pennsylvania Avenue, just across the street from the White House. After Jackson's retirement in 1837, Blair became a close adviser to the new president, Martin Van Buren, who had also been a member of the Kitchen Cabinet. Even after the victory of Whig William Henry Harrison in 1840, Blair used his editorship of the *Globe* to rally Democratic opposition. James K. Polk, however, was no admirer of Blair; and when Young Hickory became president in 1845, he forced Blair's resignation from the *Globe*.

Leasing his city residence to a series of cabinet members, the disgruntled fifty-four-year-old Blair retired to Silver Spring, Maryland, where he had recently constructed a large country estate. In 1852, however, Blair reoccupied his Washington residence (known as Blair House), and was soon joined there by his oldest son, Montgomery, who had been working as a lawyer, judge, and U.S. attorney in Missouri.

Although Blair kept several slaves in his household, he saw that slavery had no national future and thus sided with the Free Soil wing of the Democrat party, which attempted to nominate Van Buren for president in 1848. Out of residual loyalty, Blair stuck with the party, reluctantly supporting Franklin Pierce in 1852, but that would be the last time. In 1854, he helped organize the new Republican party and in February 1856 presided over its first national convention. With Abraham Lincoln's election in 1860, Blair completed his comeback and resumed his cherished role as presidential neighbor and confidant. "Father Blair," Lincoln called him.

MONTGOMERY BLAIR

Postmaster General

PORTRAYED BY BYRON JENNINGS

MONTGOMERY Blair was seventeen years old when his father—Francis Preston Blair, Sr.—moved the family to the nation's capital to serve Pres. Andrew Jackson. A year later, when Blair turned eighteen, Old Hickory gave the naturally contentious young man a gift, a coveted presidential appointment to the U.S. Military Academy at West Point, which he accepted.

Following his 1835 graduation and a year fighting the Seminoles in Florida, the twenty-three-year-old Blair moved out to St. Louis, where he prepared for the law under the tutelage of his father's close political ally Thomas Hart Benton, the powerful senator from Missouri. Both Benton and the Blairs considered slavery an evil to be tolerated where it already existed but in no case to be extended to new areas, such as the western territories.

Aided by his father's connections, Blair rose quickly. In 1839, two years after his admission to the bar, he became the U.S. attorney for Missouri. Six years after that, he became a judge. In 1855, after moving back to Washington, he was appointed the first solicitor general to the new U.S. Court of Claims. As one of the top lawyers in the capital during this period, Blair argued numerous cases before the Supreme Court, including the notorious *Dred Scott v. Sandford* (1857).

Serving pro bono as Dred Scott's counsel, Blair presented the uncontested facts. Scott, a slave, had once been owned by an army surgeon. During the course of the surgeon's military career, he repeatedly took Scott with him into free states and territories. Numerous legal precedents held that slaves traveling with their owners onto free soil immediately became free themselves. The Supreme Court, however, by a vote of 7–2, reached a different conclusion. In a majority opinion written by Chief Justice Roger B. Taney of Maryland, the Court held that Scott and all other Negroes, free and enslaved, were not and never had been U.S. citizens. Therefore, being inferior, "they had no rights which the white man was bound to respect."

Taney expected that, with this single blow, his opinion would win the slavery fight for the South. Instead, the Court's egregiously one-sided decision merely provoked Northerners into flouting the justices' authority. "This decision, we need hardly say," Horace Greeley editorialized in the *New York Tribune*, "is entitled to just so much moral weight as would be the judgment of a majority of those congregated in any Washington bar-room."

ELIZABETH BLAIR

Daughter of Francis Preston Blair, Sr.

PORTRAYED BY JULIE WHITE

JUST twelve years old at the time, Elizabeth Blair was exhilarated by her family's move from Frankfort, Kentucky, to Washington. She especially enjoyed sitting beside her father as he discussed politics endlessly with Pres. Andrew Jackson. Because she was often called upon to transcribe correspondence and other documents, Francis Preston Blair, Sr., liked to say that his daughter was "brought up in caucus."

The childless Jackson developed a special affection for the bright, savvy teenager and shared her family's concern for her often poor health. One winter, when excessive dampness in the Blair home caused her to become ill, Jackson insisted that she stay with him in the White House until conditions improved.

By the time Jackson left office in 1837, the nineteen-year-old Blair had grown into an attractive, vivacious, and self-possessed young woman. Personable, witty, and politically connected, she moved about Washington at the highest levels and became a much-sought-after social prize. All the balls and theater outings, however, taxed her still-frail constitution and made it necessary for her to take frequent trips to Appalachian spas to recover her strength.

In August 1839, during one of these trips to White Sulphur Springs in western Virginia, she met and fell in love with a twenty-seven-year-old navy lieutenant named Samuel Phillips Lee. Although Lee belonged to one of Virginia's most prominent families—his grandfather Richard Henry Lee had signed the Declaration of Independence—Preston Blair took a strong dislike to him and opposed the match, even contriving a trip to miss his daughter's 1843 wedding. With the passage of time, however, the relationship healed, and in 1859 Preston Blair built a home for the couple next door to his own at 1653 Pennsylvania Avenue.

During the Civil War, Elizabeth Blair Lee wrote hundreds of letters to her husband, who was often away at sea, having been promoted to rear admiral and placed in charge of the North Atlantic Blockading Squadron in 1862. Her long, detailed epistles, filled with an insider's knowledge of the capital's political and social life, have become important historical resources. "Lincoln is a good true man & is doing a good work for his country & earning great renown for himself," she wrote to her husband in June 1861. "His cool way of doing things will I hope teach the Blairs a lesson not to rush at things or people so violently."

THADDEUS STEVENS

Radical Republican Representative of Pennsylvania

PORTRAYED BY TOMMY LEE JONES

WHEN Henry Winter Davis returned to Washington for the first session of the Thirty-eighth Congress in December 1863, one of his first chores was to visit Thaddeus Stevens, the powerful, cantankerous chairman of the House Ways and Means Committee. "I called in the committee of Ways and Means room to see old Stevens," Davis wrote to his friend Rear Adm. Samuel F. Du Pont. "Grim, savage, sarcastic, mordant as ever—living on brandy & opium to subdue perpetual pain & mocking at the powers that be in the most spicy way."

At seventy-one, Stevens had already lived a long and successful life, if not a particularly happy or healthy one. His club foot had prevented him from joining the Masons (they didn't accept "cripples"), and a subsequent bout of "brain fever" (alopecia) had left him hairless, requiring that he wear a wig (its dark color, compared to his pale skin, often made him seem corpselike). Despite his many achievements, Stevens was generally an embittered man who believed that he could have achieved even more had others not denied him the even loftier positions to which he was entitled.

During the 1830s, Stevens served several terms in the Pennsylvania state legislature, often championing the rights of African Americans. A staunch abolitionist, he helped runaway slaves escape the country via the Underground Railroad and, as a lawyer, defended those who were captured in court. In 1837–38, he served as a delegate to the state constitutional convention, refusing to sign the final document because it denied the right of suffrage to black men. After moving from Gettysburg to Lancaster in 1842, he served two undistinguished terms in Congress before retiring from politics at the age of sixty-one. In 1858, however, as the struggle over slavery intensified, Stevens heeded the call of conscience and returned to the House, where he served until his death in August 1868.

According to Pennsylvania journalist and politician Alexander K. McClure, "Stevens was the one man who never faltered, who never hesitated, who never temporized, who was ready to meet aggressive treason with the most aggressive assaults. He and Lincoln worked substantially on the same lines, earnestly striving to attain the same ends, but Stevens was always in advance of public sentiment, while Lincoln ever halted until assured that the considerate judgment of the nation would sustain him."

JAMES ASHLEY

Radical Republican Representative of Ohio

✦ ✦ ✦

PORTRAYED BY DAVID COSTABILE

ALTHOUGH James Ashley certainly admired Pres. Abraham Lincoln, his true political patron was Secretary of the Treasury Salmon P. Chase. A fellow Ohioan, Chase had joined forces with the much younger Ashley in 1854, when Chase first decided to seek the 1855 gubernatorial nomination of the infant Republican party. Chase valued Ashley's strong commitments to both abolition and temperance (then a growing force in Ohio politics), and he provided in return not only a compelling social vision but also a much needed father figure to Ashley, whose life up to that point had been mostly rudderless.

By the mid-1850s, Ashley had already cut off relations with his father, an itinerant Campbellite minister who was as unstable as he was dogmatic. The family's incessant wanderings through Illinois, Kentucky, and the Ohio Valley had made it impossible for Ashley to attend school, so in the mode of Lincoln he educated himself. As a young man, he worked on the Mississippi as a riverboat deck hand and stevedore, later becoming a printer and editor of Democratic newspapers. Meanwhile, he studied law, gaining admission to the bar in 1849 at the age of twenty-four. But Ashley never became a practicing attorney; instead, he turned to the wholesale drug business.

Along with the publicity skills he had developed in the newspaper business, Ashley's previous political lives as a Democrat and briefly as a Know-Nothing helped Chase win the Republican gubernatorial nomination and later the general election. Three years later, with the support of now-Governor Chase, Ashley ran for congress and won the first of four consecutive terms.

Not surprisingly, Representative Ashley refused to consider any compromises over slavery or secession. When in December 1860 desperate House members voted overwhelmingly to create a Committee of Thirty-three (one member from each state) to consider compromises that might avert civil war, Ashley cast one of the thirty-eight nays.

Ashley also fought the result of the committee's work, a convoluted constitutional amendment that would have banned future amendments banning slavery. The House passed the measure, known as the Corwin Amendment, on March 2, 1861, by a two-thirds majority of those members voting (many Southern representatives having already vacated their seats). Ashley argued unsuccessfully that passage required a two-thirds majority of all House members. Four years later, however, when the Thirteenth Amendment came up for a vote, Ashley (who acted as that amendment's floor manager in the House) benefitted greatly from the precedent set in 1861.

GEORGE PENDLETON

Democratic Representative of Ohio

. . .

PORTRAYED BY PETER McROBBIE

GEORGE H. Pendleton belonged to one of Cincinnati's most prominent families. His grandfather, an aide-de-camp to Nathanael Greene during the Revolutionary War, became a federal judge and was Alexander Hamilton's second in his famous duel with Aaron Burr. Pendleton's father served two terms in the Ohio state senate and one in the U.S. House.

The sixteen-year-old Pendleton graduated from Cincinnati College (a secondary school) in 1841 and three years later set off for Europe, where he traveled extensively and studied for a time at Heidelberg University. Upon his return to Cincinnati in 1846, Pendleton married Alice Key, daughter of Francis Scott Key and niece of Chief Justice of the Supreme Court Roger B. Taney. A year later, he was admitted to the bar and began practicing law. In 1853, he followed his father into politics, winning election to the state senate as a Democrat. Pendleton failed in his first bid for congress in 1854 but won election two years later and served four consecutive terms. As a member of the House, he backed Stephen Douglas' theory of popular sovereignty and opposed any measure that would ban slavery in the western territories.

During the Civil War, Pendleton became a leader of the Peace Democrats (Copperheads), whose influence within the Northern Democratic party was considerable. In fact, the Copperheads wielded so much power at the 1864 Democratic National Convention that they forced presidential nominee George B. McClellan, a War Democrat, to accept the thirty-nine-year-old Pendleton as his vice presidential running mate. Unfortunately, in November, Pendleton lost both the national election and his House seat. It was thus as a lame duck that he led the opposition to the Thirteenth Amendment in January 1865.

After 1865, Pendleton's national importance waned, but he remained an influential figure in Ohio. In 1878, the state legislature elected him to the Senate, where he introduced the Pendleton Civil Service Reform Act of 1883. This landmark legislation outlawed the corrupt "spoils system" by which generations of elected officials had awarded government jobs to political cronies rather than to the most qualified applicants. Unhappy with the resulting decline in their patronage, the members of the Ohio state legislature declined to reelect Pendleton in 1884; but Pres. Grover Cleveland, who had supported civil service reform, rewarded Pendleton with the post of U.S. minister to Germany.

FERNANDO WOOD

Democratic Representative of New York

✦ ✦ ✦

PORTRAYED BY LEE PACE

FERNANDO Wood didn't have a good public reputation. In New York City, where he lived, most people thought he was a crook. During the 1830s and 1840s, he made a fortune in shipping and land speculation. Word was, however, that most of his money came from cheating investors. A fraud conviction during the California Gold Rush didn't help.

Despite this reputation, Wood decided to enter politics. He joined Tammany Hall, the city's powerful Democratic machine, and used his wealth to obtain a top leadership position. During this time, he mentored future Tammany leader William M. Tweed. "I never went to get a corner lot," the famously corrupt Boss Tweed once remarked, "that I didn't find Wood had got in ahead of me." Manipulating the rapidly expanding immigrant vote, Wood captured the mayoralty in 1854 and won reelection two years later. His only noteworthy achievement during these two terms was to veto legislation that would have reduced the size of the future Central Park. Wood did try to improve his reputation by backing a number of municipal reforms, presumably on the theory that it takes a crook to know a crook; but none of these measures passed.

Meanwhile, he angered his erstwhile friends at Tammany Hall by failing to provide the expected patronage. (Rumor had it that the mayor was selling city jobs and contracts to the highest bidders). As a result, Wood lost the election of 1857 but was unbowed. He founded his own Democratic organization, Mozart Hall, and returned to office in 1860.

Fiercely pro-Southern, Wood was New York City's leading defender of slavery, not only because he profited personally as a middleman in the cotton trade but also because of his own conspicuous racism. Two weeks after South Carolina seceded, Wood recommended to the common council that New York City secede as well so that it could continue trading with all comers as a "free city." In 1862, he won a seat in Congress as a Peace Democrat and later opposed the Thirteenth Amendment.

Years after Wood's death, political rival John Bigelow happened to be visiting City Hall when he passed a portrait of Wood in the hallway. Pausing to inspect the likeness, the former U.S. minister to France observed, "He was the handsomest man I ever saw, and the most corrupt man that ever sat in the mayor's chair."

GEORGE YEAMAN

Unionist Representative of Kentucky

‡ ‡ ‡

PORTRAYED BY MICHAEL STUHLBARG

NO DOUBT Abraham Lincoln saw something of himself in George Helm Yeaman. Although twenty years the president's junior, Yeaman had, like Lincoln, been born in hardscrabble Hardin County, Kentucky, to a struggling family of questionable means. Also like Lincoln, Yeaman had received little formal education but nevertheless chose to make something of himself by studying law on his own.

While Lincoln's family moved north across the Ohio River in search of greater economic opportunity, Yeaman moved only so far as neighboring Daviess County. After gaining admission to the bar in 1852, Yeaman began practicing law in Owensboro, the county seat. Within two years, he was serving as judge of Daviess County while also editing the *Owensboro Gazette*.

A member of the Whig party until its collapse in the mid-1850s, Yeaman remained strongly Unionist, supporting Constitutional Union party candidate John Bell in the 1860 election. That winter, as civil war neared, Yeaman opposed secession for Kentucky and joined a Unionist slate of candidates that won control of the state legislature in August 1861. A year later, voters sent Yeaman to Washington to fill the congressional seat vacated by James S. Jackson when he resigned to join the Union army. (Jackson was later killed commanding a division at Perryville.)

Like most of the War Democrats with whom he became allied, Yeaman had no quarrel with slavery, only with secession. Immediately upon his arrival in Washington, he introduced a resolution condemning the recently issued Preliminary Emancipation Proclamation as "not warranted by the Constitution" and "an assumption of power dangerous to the rights of citizens and to the perpetuity of a free people." When the House initially voted on the Thirteenth Amendment in June 1864, Yeaman was among the amendment's opponents. But when the amendment came up for a second vote in January 1865, Lincoln decided to intervene personally.

The president knew that the thirty-five-year-old congressman had lost his bid for reelection and must be looking for new opportunities. No one knows what the two men said to each other during their private discussions, but Yeaman changed his mind, voting aye on January 31; and seven months later, Secretary of State William Seward appointed him U.S. minister to Denmark, a comfortable position in which Yeaman served five years.

ALEXANDER COFFROTH

Democratic Representative of Pennsylvania

✦ ✦ ✦

PORTRAYED BY BORIS MCGIVER

ALTHOUGH Somerset County in Pennsylvania, where Alexander Coffroth was raised, had a majority Republican population, Coffroth himself was a Democrat. From the age of eighteen, he edited a local Democratic journal called the *Somerset Visitor*; and about the same time, he began reading law with Jeremiah S. Black, an up-and-coming Democratic attorney. In 1851, the same year that Coffroth gained admission to the bar, Black became chief justice of the Pennsylvania Supreme Court. Six years later, Black moved to Washington, where he served fellow Pennsylvanian James Buchanan first as attorney general and then as secretary of state.

In April 1860, Coffroth attended the Democratic National Convention in Charleston, South Carolina, as a delegate. Angrily, he watched his party split over the issue of slavery. As a staunch Unionist, Coffroth supported Illinois senator Stephen A. Douglas; and when the Northern wing of the party reconvened in Baltimore two months later, he joined the other delegates in nominating the Little Giant by a unanimous voice vote.

Like many War Democrats, Coffroth benefitted from the initially adverse reaction to Lincoln's Emancipation Proclamation, winning a seat in Congress in the 1862 midterm elections. Coffroth's signature issues were conscription and emancipation, both of which he opposed. Although not a fan of slavery, Coffroth was deeply concerned that freed blacks would eventually migrate to the North.

Coffroth became a key player in the Thirteenth Amendment fight for two reasons: first, he and Lincoln were friends (Coffroth later served as a pallbearer at the president's funeral); and, second, his 1864 reelection victory (by a margin of seventy-three votes) was being contested. According to the story that later went around Washington, the Republican leadership promised Coffroth his seat in the next Congress if he agreed to vote aye on the amendment.

Coffroth indeed voted aye, causing the *Harrisburg Patriot and Union* to call him a "stool pigeon . . . ready at any moment to take his anxious flight to the [Republicans'] well-filled feed-troughs." But he did get his seat, if only temporarily. In February 1866, the Republican-dominated House voted to seat Coffroth while his reelection continued to be contested. Five months later, however, when a commission decided the race in favor of Republican William H. Koontz, Coffroth was ousted. He returned to Somerset County, where Andrew Johnson appointed him an assessor of internal revenue in 1867.

ALEXANDER H. STEPHENS

Vice President of the Confederate States of America

◆ ◆

PORTRAYED BY JACKIE EARLE HALEY

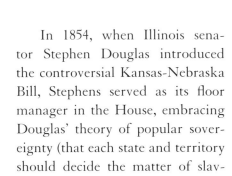

ALEXANDER Hamilton Stephens made two impressions on the lawmakers he met. The first related to his size—or lack thereof. Weighing just ninety pounds, Stephens was a short, frail man, tubercular in appearance and never in good health. When he spoke, however, he made a second impression that was the more lasting.

Abraham Lincoln became friendly with Little Ellick, as Stephens was called, when both men were Whig members of the House. In February 1848, two months into his first congressional session, Lincoln wrote to a friend, "I just take up my pen to say, that Mr. Stephens of Georgia, a little slim, pale faced, consumptive man, . . . has just concluded the very best speech, of an hour's length, I ever heard. My old, withered, dry eyes, are full of tears yet."

A Unionist in spite of his staunchly proslavery views, Stephens worked closely with Lincoln and other Northern Whigs to elect party presidential nominee Zachary Taylor in 1848. As the sectional crisis intensified, however, the Whig party became unstable and ultimately collapsed. Initially, Stephens helped found a new moderate Southern party, the Constitutional Unionists, but this effort proved short lived. By 1852, Stephens had no practical choice but to join the Democrats.

In 1854, when Illinois senator Stephen Douglas introduced the controversial Kansas-Nebraska Bill, Stephens served as its floor manager in the House, embracing Douglas' theory of popular sovereignty (that each state and territory should decide the matter of slavery for itself). "I feel as if the Mission of my life was performed," the Georgian wrote soon after the bill's passage.

In 1860, Stephens supported the Illinois senator's campaign for the presidency even though most Southern Democrats despised Douglas for defeating a platform plank that would have rejected popular sovereignty in favor of a guarantee that slavery would be protected throughout the nation. The fire-eaters' strategy, Stephens concluded, was "rule or ruin."

After Lincoln's election in November, Stephens fought vigorously to keep Georgia in the Union. When secession came nevertheless in January 1861, the retired congressman felt honor bound to accept the will of the majority. He was elected to the Provisional Confederate Congress, which met in Montgomery, Alabama, in early February 1861. Competing for the presidency, Stephens lost to Jefferson Davis; but he was subsequently made vice president in the hope that his election would encourage other moderates to support the new government.

PART TWO

THE ROAD TO
THE THIRTEENTH
AMENDMENT

I claim not to have controlled events,

but confess plainly that events have controlled me.

—ABRAHAM LINCOLN

I

And the War Came

DURING the winter of 1840–41, Abraham Lincoln suffered a depression so severe that close friends considered him potentially suicidal. Two dismal events combined to bring on this black emotional state: the collapse of his engagement to Mary Todd and the decision of his closest friend, Joshua Speed, to leave Springfield. Like Lincoln, Speed was a native Kentuckian, and the recent death of his father had persuaded him that it was time to return home to care for the family plantation.

"I am now the most miserable man living," Lincoln wrote to John Todd Stuart, his law partner and Mary's cousin, on January 23, 1841. "If what I feel were equally distributed to the whole human family, there would not be one cheerful face on the earth. Whether I shall ever be better I can not tell; I awfully forebode I shall not. To remain as I am is impossible; I must die or be better, it appears to me."

Lincoln had stopped attending sessions of the Illinois state legislature, of which he was an influential member, and even ceased getting out of bed. "As I now

Mary Todd Lincoln as she appeared in late 1846 or early 1847, about the time of her twenty-eighth birthday.

remember," fellow legislator Orville H. Browning recalled, "his derangement lasted only about a week or such a matter. He was so much affected as to talk incoherently, and to be delirious to the extent of not knowing what he was doing."

Speed's memory was even sharper. "Lincoln went crazy," he wrote in response to an interviewer's question not long after the president's death. "Had to remove razors from his room—take away all knives and other such dangerous things—&c—it was terrible."

Speed became so concerned that he finally warned Lincoln he would die if he didn't rally. "I am not afraid, and would be more than willing," Lincoln replied. "But I have an irrepressible desire to live till I can be assured that the world is a little better for my having lived in it."

Years later, both men recalled this moment as a cusp in Lincoln's life. It was Lincoln's long-held ambition to make a mark upon history, they agreed—to be remembered fondly by future generations—that rescued him from his deep despair.

BECAUSE Lincoln has since come to occupy such an exalted place in the national memory, it can be difficult to recall that, prior to his election as president, he failed

OPPOSITE: **This daguerreotype, the earliest known photograph of Abraham Lincoln, was taken in Springfield, Illinois, shortly after Lincoln's 1846 election to Congress.**

Secretary of State
William H. Seward

Treasury Secretary
Salmon P. Chase

Attorney General
Edward Bates

in politics more than he succeeded. In 1854–55 and again in 1858–59, he ran for seats in the U.S. Senate and lost both times, first to Lyman Trumbull and then to Stephen Douglas. When Lincoln decided to seek the presidential nomination of the relatively new Republican party in 1860, he was considered the fourth most likely candidate to win—out of a field of four.

Of the three other candidates—Edward Bates of Missouri, Salmon P. Chase of Ohio, and William H. Seward of New York—Seward was the clear front-runner, yet his nomination was far from certain. He faced strong opposition from some key party constituencies—including conservative Republicans, who objected to his strong anti-slavery views, and nativists, who didn't approve of his tolerance of immigrants. Going into the Chicago convention, Lincoln's strategy was to consolidate his support among the western delegations while positioning himself to be everyone else's second choice. (In 1860, his home state of Illinois was still considered to be on the western frontier.) Lincoln's hope was that the opposition to Seward would coalesce, at which point the convention would have to seek a compromise alternative—someone who was a moderate and too obscure to have made many enemies—in other words, himself.

On the question of slavery, the central issue of the election, Lincoln was indeed a moderate—for a

Republican, that is. Like every other member of his party, he believed that under no circumstances should the South's "peculiar institution" be allowed to expand into the western territories.

The Republican party was formed in 1854 following passage of the Kansas-Nebraska Act, which carved two new territories out of still-unorganized Louisiana Purchase land. The bill's proximate purpose was economic—to increase settlement and encourage development of a transcontinental railroad—but the inescapable question of whether the new territories would permit slavery made the legislation highly contentious.

Disputes between North and South over slavery were certainly nothing new. Since 1787, when the framers of the Constitution agreed on the ugly compromise that counted each Southern slave as three-fifths of a human being (for purposes of taxation and representation), the two regions had regularly come into conflict over how the nation's labor system should be organized. A notable episode began in 1819, when the House of Representatives approved a bill granting residents of the Missouri Territory, many of whom owned slaves, permission to draft a state constitution (a prerequisite for admission to the Union). To assure passage, however, the Southern sponsors of the bill had to accept a Northern amendment prohibiting the introduction of more slaves into Missouri and setting free the children of existing slaves when they turned twenty-five. When Southerners in the Senate balked at these terms, the admission of Missouri turned into a constitutional debate.

Antislavery Northerners argued that, while the Constitution admittedly protected slavery in states where it already existed, no provision in the document barred the federal government from excluding slavery in new states and territories. Slaveholding Southerners responded that new states should enjoy the same sovereignty rights as existing ones and therefore be able to decide the matter for themselves.

The constitutional argument was never resolved, but a political accommodation was eventually reached. The practical core of the issue was control of the Senate, where the eleven slave and eleven free states shared power with twenty-two votes each (two per state). Admitting Missouri, either as a free state or as a slave state, would upset that perfect balance, giving a decisive advantage to one region or the other. In early 1820, however, the territory of Maine also petitioned for admission, creating the possibility for a deal. According to the arrangement brokered by Speaker of the House Henry Clay, Missouri and Maine would be admitted simultaneously—the former as a slave state, the latter as a free state. That way, the balance of power in the Senate would be preserved.

Yet the admission of Maine as a free state wasn't enough to satisfy Northerners, who insisted that slavery's northward expansion be restricted. So Clay included a provision in the legislation establishing a line at latitude 36° 30' N. South of that line within the Louisiana

The artist who painted this 1852 scene of an American slave market is known only by his surname, Taylor.

Purchase, slavery would be permitted. In all Louisiana Purchase land north of that line, with the exception of Missouri itself, slavery would be banned.

The Missouri Compromise held until the early 1850s, when the need to organize territories in Kansas and Nebraska revived the issue. Lincoln's views were typical of the Northern moderate mainstream. On a personal level, he considered slavery an immoral practice and preferred it abolished. As a politician, however, he recognized that this wasn't possible under the Constitution, and he accepted that reality. Nevertheless, he was determined on moral grounds to prevent slavery's westward expansion.

Containing slavery to the states where it already existed, Lincoln believed, would undermine the Southern economy and eventually cause slavery to collapse of its own weight. The Southerners who controlled the Democratic party during the 1850s agreed with Lincoln's assessment— that slavery would die if contained—so they pressed hard for its expansion. Among the hurdles they faced was the Missouri Compromise itself, which disallowed slavery in

Antislavery Kansans were nicknamed Jayhawks. This group was photographed in Lawrence in 1859.

Kansas and Nebraska because both lay north of the 36° 30' N line.

Given the popular reverence for this time-tested compromise, the Democrats should have had a difficult time winning its repeal. But in 1854, the Democratic party's erstwhile national rival, the Whig party, was nearing the end of its existence. Before the country's eyes, it was disintegrating along sectional lines into "cotton Whigs," who sympathized with the slaveholding South, and "conscience Whigs," who sought abolition on moral grounds. Moreover, Southern Democrats were finding a great deal of support among racist Northerners who agreed with the Southern defense of states' rights. To emphasize this national reach, the Democratic party took to nominating Northerners for president, selecting Franklin Pierce of New Hampshire in 1852 and James Buchanan of Pennsylvania in 1856. In the parlance of the time, these men were known as doughfaces, because their political

I HAD for a long time ceased to read the newspapers or pay any attention to public affairs, confident they were in good hands, and content to be a passenger in our bark to the shore from which I am not distant. But this momentous question, like a fire bell in the night, awakened and filled me with terror. I considered it at once as the knell of the Union. It is hushed indeed for the moment. But this is a reprieve only, not a final sentence. A geographical line, coinciding with a marked principle, moral and political, once conceived and held up to the angry passions of men, will never be obliterated; and every new irritation will mark it deeper and deeper.

—THOMAS JEFFERSON
(Discussing the Missouri Compromise in a letter to
Rep. John Holmes, April 22, 1820)

features were sufficiently malleable to suit Southern tastes.

Following Pierce's decisive win over Whig nominee Winfield Scott in the 1852 election, the Democrats moved on Kansas and Nebraska. Illinois senator Stephen Douglas wrote the legislation, which supplanted the Missouri Compromise with the logic of "popular sovereignty"—that is, the principle that the residents of a state or territory should be able to decide for themselves whether or not to permit slavery. Pierce signed the Kansas-Nebraska Act into law on May 30, 1854, beginning the era of Bleeding Kansas. During this seven-year period, anti- and proslavery settlers battled one another figuratively and literally for political control of the territory.

Meanwhile, it became obvious to opponents of slavery nationwide that, with the demise of the Whig organization, they would have to create a new national party if they were going to challenge the sway of the Democrats. Thus, in rather short order, conscience Whigs united with antislavery Democrats (known as Free Soilers) to form the Republican party, which Lincoln (a conscience Whig) joined in 1855.

ABRAHAM Lincoln was in many ways a humble man, but he never lacked confidence in himself or in his ability to lead. This gave him an unusual strength. For example, when he was elected president in 1860, he resisted the common temptation to appoint like-minded people to his cabinet. Instead, he named his erstwhile opponents—Seward as secretary of state, Chase as secretary of the treasury, and Bates as attorney general. Never before had an American president (with the possible exception of George Washington) been so open to exchanging influence for consensus. Yet Lincoln wasn't being altogether magnanimous. With the South moving toward secession, he knew that he must do all he could to hold the disparate elements of the Republican party together.

During the 1860 campaign—which had been a four-way race among Lincoln, Douglas (the choice of the Northern Democrats), John

Breckinridge (the nominee of the Southern Democrats), and John Bell (a border-state Unionist)—supporters of Breckinridge had warned repeatedly that they would consider a Lincoln victory conclusive proof that the North was unwilling to respect states' rights, especially those protecting the institution of slavery. These Southern extremists, known as fire-eaters, considered such disrespect intolerable—and, true to their word, when Lincoln indeed won the election (with less than 40 percent of the popular vote), they demanded secession.

South Carolina, which had been resisting the exercise of federal power since the 1820s, became the first state to leave the Union, approving an ordinance of secession on December 20, 1860. During January, Mississippi, Florida, Alabama, Georgia, and Louisiana (in that order) followed South Carolina's example. On February 4, delegates from these six states met in Montgomery, Alabama, to draft a constitution for the new Confederate States of America. They also elected the Confederacy's first (and only) president, Jefferson Davis of Mississippi. In early March, Texas joined the Confederacy.

This 1860 presidential campaign cartoon depicts the four candidates—John Bell, Stephen A. Douglas, John C. Breckinridge, and Abraham Lincoln—as baseball players.

THE NATIONAL GAME. THREE "OUTS" AND ONE "RUN".
ABRAHAM WINNING THE BALL.

Reaction in the North was split. Some pundits, such as *New York Tribune* editor Horace Greeley, advocated passivity. In an editorial published on the day that South Carolina began formal consideration of the secession ordinance, the powerful Republican opinion shaper opined that the North should simply let the Southern states go. Otherwise, Northerners would be violating the core principle enunciated by Jefferson in the Declaration of Independence that governments derive their legitimacy from the consent of the governed:

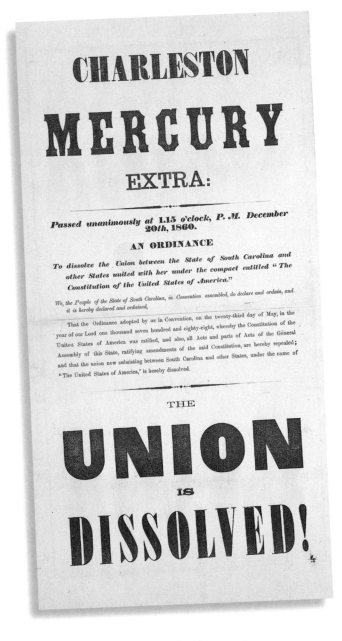

This special edition of the *Charleston Mercury* announced the December 20, 1860, secession of South Carolina.

If seven or eight contiguous States shall present themselves authentically at Washington, saying, "We hate the Federal Union; we have withdrawn from it; we give you the choice between acquiescing in our secession and arranging amicably all incidental questions on the one hand, and attempting to subdue us on the other"—we could not stand up for coercion, for subjugation, for we do not think it would be just. We hold the right of Self-Government sacred, even when invoked in behalf of those who deny it to others.

Other Northern factions had different viewpoints. One sought reconciliation with—that is, appeasement of—the South in order to preserve lucrative commerce between the two regions. Another wanted the U.S. Army to invade the South immediately and force its submission. These and other opinions were debated daily in the ubiquitous newspapers that were the nineteenth century's primary media. But there was a crucial unknown. No one yet knew what Abraham Lincoln would do when he took office on March 4. Quite reasonably, many wondered whether the untested frontier lawyer would measure up to the challenge.

Lincoln's 1861 inauguration was a somber affair. His audience was small and not at all festive. Having learned of a plausible assassination threat against the president-elect's life, General-in-Chief Winfield Scott had deployed cannon to guard strategic points around Washington and posted sharpshooters to monitor the crowd at the Capitol.

The inaugural address that Lincoln delivered was precisely balanced, expressing both his resolve to defend the Union and his hope for an amicable resolution to the crisis. He began by addressing, and attempting to relieve, what he perceived to be the most troubling Southern anxieties. "I have no purpose, directly or indirectly, to interfere with the institution of slavery in the States where it exists," he said. "I believe I have no lawful right to do so, and I have no inclination to do so."

Lincoln went on, however, to make it clear that he would not countenance secession: "If the United States be not a government proper, but an association of States in the nature of contract merely, can it, as a contract, be peaceably unmade by less than all the parties who made it? One party to a contract may violate it—break it, so to speak—but does it not require all to lawfully rescind it?"

Standing beneath the wooden canopy on the steps of the Capitol, Lincoln takes part in his first inauguration.

The address was typical of the rhetorical style that always won Lincoln admirers among those who listened to him. As was often the case, the speech made use of a familiar analogue (a legal contract) to break down for the audience a complicated idea (the relationship of the individual states to the Union).

"I therefore consider," Lincoln said, "that in view of the Constitution and the laws, the Union is unbroken, and to the extent of my ability, I shall take care, as the Constitution itself expressly enjoins upon me, that the laws of the Union be faithfully executed in all the states."

This point being made, the new president returned to his initial, reassuring tone. "In doing this there needs to be no bloodshed or violence, and there shall be none unless it be forced upon the national authority," he explained. "The power confided to me will be used to hold, occupy, and possess the property and places belonging to the Government and to collect the duties and imposts; but beyond what may be necessary for these objects, there will be no invasion, no using of force against or among the people anywhere."

Even so, Lincoln knew that many in the South, especially in militant South Carolina, were eager for war;

Lincoln personally edited this printed draft of his first inaugural address. The inset shows the famous concluding lines he added before delivering the speech.

I AM loath to close. We are not enemies, but friends. We must not be enemies. Though passion may have strained it must not break our bonds of affection. The mystic chords of memory, stretching from every battlefield and patriot grave to every living heart and hearthstone all over this broad land, will yet swell the chorus of the Union, when again touched, as surely they will be, by the better angels of our nature.

—ABRAHAM LINCOLN
(First inaugural address, March 4, 1861)

and that, despite his own efforts for peace, it might well come. Therefore, he concluded his speech with a reference to Southern belligerence intended to make the historical record clear. "In your hands, my dissatisfied fellow-countrymen, and not in mine, is the momentous issue of civil war," he said. "The Government will not assail you. You have no conflict without being yourselves the aggressors."

THE flashpoint, everyone knew, was Fort Sumter, a federal garrison on a small island in Charleston Bay. If the new president was going to keep his inaugural promise to "hold, occupy, and possess" all federal property in the South, he would have to resupply Fort Sumter—and soon.

Until December 20, the fort's quartermaster had routinely purchased provisions for the troops from local merchants; with secession, however, that was no longer possible. In early January 1861, the Buchanan administration dispatched a civilian ship, the *Star of the West*, to attempt a resupply. But as the ship entered Charleston Bay on January 9, cadets from the Citadel stationed on nearby Morris Island fired on the *Star of the West*, forcing its retreat.

When Lincoln took office on March 4, the garrison had about six weeks' worth of rations left. If the president was indeed going to hold Fort Sumter, he would have to resupply it using much more resolve than his doughface predecessor had shown. Yet there were significant limits, both practical and political, to what Lincoln could do. At the time, the armed forces available to him were small and demobilized, hardly enough to overcome the massed strength of the "home team" South Carolinians. Even more importantly, the political fate of the Upper South— Virginia, North Carolina, Kentucky, and Tennessee—was still undecided. All four states were currently considering secession ordinances, and Lincoln feared that shooting in South Carolina would tip them into the Confederate fold. On April 6, after five weeks in office, the president sent

This 1861 Currier & Ives lithograph shows the Confederate bombardment of Fort Sumter in Charleston Harbor.

a message to South Carolina governor Francis Pickens, informing Pickens of Lincoln's intention to resupply Sumter with food and water only. Should this mission proceed peacefully, Lincoln promised, no troop reinforcements would follow. After receiving Lincoln's message on April 8, Pickens immediately informed Brig. Gen. P. G. T. Beauregard, commander of the Confederate forces in Charleston. Beauregard, in turn, communicated the content of the message to the Confederate War Department, which ordered Beauregard to demand Sumter's surrender "at once . . . and if this is refused proceed, in such manner as you may determine, to reduce it." On April 11, Beauregard dutifully sent three officers to the fort to demand its surrender. The fort's commander, Maj. Robert Anderson, refused. Consequently, at half past four in the morning on April 12, the Confederate shore batteries opened fire on Sumter.

With the outbreak of hostilities, Virginia, Arkansas, Tennessee, and finally North Carolina seceded from the Union and joined their Southern brethren in the Confederacy. "Both parties deprecated war," Lincoln later observed in his second inaugural address, "but one of them would make war rather than let the nation survive; and the other would accept war rather than let it perish. And the war came."

IT was not a war to end slavery—at least not at first. As the poet Walt Whitman (who served as a nurse in a Washington military hospital) explained, if "*slavery and quiet* could have been submitted to a direct popular vote, as against their opposite, they would have triumphantly carried the day in a majority of the northern States—in the large cities, leading off with New York and Philadelphia, by tremendous majorities." Yet Northerners, unwilling to fight for an end to slavery, were willing to fight for the preservation of the Union.

It's important to understand that their conception of Union was quite different from ours today. In 1861, the United States was still a relatively young nation and still the world's most notable experiment in self-government. To Unionists such as Lincoln, dissolution meant the collapse of that experiment, threatening the cause of democracy worldwide. Although not yet willing to fight for emancipation, the great majority of Northerners were willing to fight against what they believed to be a conspiracy to put down popular government.

Perhaps unavoidably, Lincoln stumbled through the first two years of the war. After the Federals lost the first major engagement at Bull Run in July 1861, the president realized that he would need

New York Tribune editor Horace Greeley

Greeley's August 19, 1862, open letter to Lincoln, headlined "The Prayer of Twenty Millions," and the president's August 22 reply.

more and better troops to fight a longer war than anyone had imagined. During the winter of 1861–62, he worked to transform the Army of the Potomac, the Union's main force in the East, into a formidable weapon. But the man he put in charge, Maj. Gen. George B. McClellan, proved to be a poor choice—a skilled organizer but an egotistical martinet and reluctant aggressor, much more interested in drilling than battle. After McClellan's highly anticipated Peninsular Campaign ended with his army being chased out of Virginia by Robert E. Lee, Lincoln removed McClellan from command in favor of Maj. Gen. John Pope.

McClellan's failure, which emphasized the overall lack of Union military progress, took its toll on Northern morale, making it difficult for the government to raise troops and imperiling the Republicans' control of Congress. With the outbreak of war, the Democratic party in the North had split into two factions: the War Democrats, who supported the use of military force to put down the rebellion; and the Peace Democrats, who sought an immediate armistice followed by a negotiated settlement with the Confederacy. Initially, the "treason" of its Southern wing had discredited the Democratic party in the North. But by August 1862, with McClellan in full retreat, it was already apparent that Northern Democrats would fare quite well in the upcoming midterm elections.

Recognizing this, Horace Greeley published an open letter to Lincoln on August 19, entitled "The Prayer of Twenty Millions." Having changed his mind about the war, the *New York Tribune* editor now wanted the president to take a more aggressive stance. Specifically, he second-guessed Lincoln's decision not to threaten emancipation in his first inaugural address. "Had you then proclaimed that Rebellion would strike the shackles from the slaves of every traitor," Greeley wrote, "the wealthy and the cautious would have been supplied with a powerful inducement to remain loyal." It was principally Lincoln's overcaution in this regard, Greeley argued, that was hobbling the Northern war effort.

"We cannot conquer Ten Millions of People united in solid phalanx against us, powerfully aided by the Northern sympathizers and European allies," Greeley concluded. "We must have scouts, guides, spies, cooks, teamsters, diggers and choppers from the Blacks of the South, whether we allow them to fight for us or not, or we shall be baffled and repelled."

Lincoln responded on August 22 with the clarity and sharpness of a fine diamond:

My paramount object in this struggle is to save the Union, and is not either to save or to destroy slavery. If I could save the Union without freeing any slave I would do it, and if I could save it by freeing all the slaves I would do it; and if I could save it by freeing some and leaving others alone I would also do that. What I do about slavery, and the colored race, I do because I believe it helps to save the Union; and what I forbear, I forbear because I do not believe it would help to save the Union. I shall do less whenever I shall believe what I am doing hurts the cause, and I shall do more whenever I shall believe doing more will help the cause. I shall try to correct errors when shown to be errors; and I shall adopt new views so fast as they shall appear to be true views.

What Lincoln didn't reveal to the nation was that he had already come to the same conclusion that Greeley had reached. For the Union to win the war, he would have to expand its war aims to include the emancipation of the Rebels' slaves.

❧

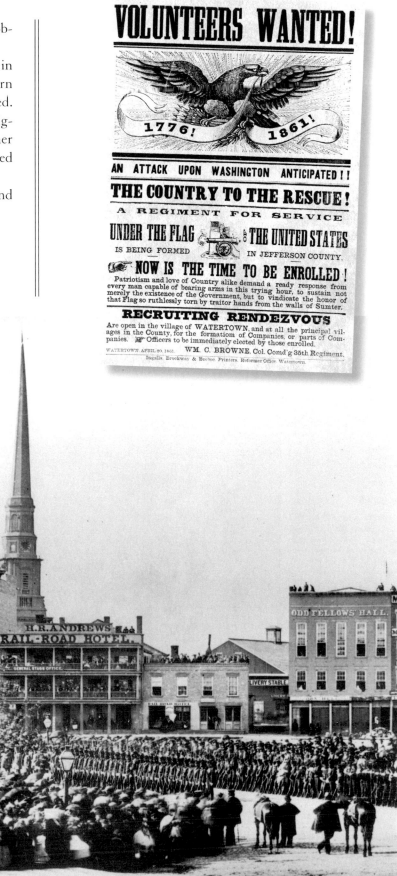

TOP: An 1861 Union recruiting poster from Watertown, Massachusetts.

RIGHT: The First Michigan Volunteer Infantry receives its regimental colors in Detroit before leaving for Washington.

II

An Indispensable Necessity

WITH the coming of war, many slaves sensed their freedom was at hand. But the course their emancipation took turned out to be much more tortuous than any could have imagined. During the first chaotic weeks of war, when confusion and doubt prevailed, a few slaves seized the opportunity to flee their masters and escape to nearby Union-held garrisons. Lacking any official guidance, the Northern officers commanding these forts weren't sure what to do with the runaways, just a trickle at first, so most continued acting as they had before the war—that is, observing the provisions of the Fugitive Slave Law and returning the slaves to their masters.

Maj. Gen. Benjamin F. Butler, commander of Fortress Monroe on the Virginia peninsula separating the Chesapeake Bay from the harborlike Hampton Roads, saw the matter differently. In May 1861, three slaves who had been put to work on Southern fortifications fled to his lines. The next day, their owner, a Confederate colonel, approached the fort under a flag of truce, demanding their return under the Fugitive Slave Law. Butler refused—pointing out that, given Virginia's declaration that it had

Waggish newspapermen described slaves who ran away, such as this contraband, as "self-emancipated."

left the Union, the Fugitive Slave Law didn't seem to apply. Instead, Butler declared the slaves "contraband of war" and put them to work in his own camp.

As news of Butler's action spread, other Union officers recognized the foolhardiness of returning slaves (and their labor) to the ranks of the enemy, and the War Department was forced to concur. For a time, officers from slaveholding border states that had remained loyal to the Union continued to return runaways; but in March 1862, Congress finally prohibited the practice.

Meanwhile, word of what Butler had done spread among the slave population as well, and what had been a trickle became a steady stream of runaways. Within two months, nearly a thousand African Americans had escaped to Fortress Monroe, becoming quite a distraction for Butler. In July 1861, he wrote to Secretary of War Simon Cameron seeking clarification of the runaways' legal status. "Are these men, women, and children slaves? Are they free?" the general asked. "If property, do they not become the property of the salvors? But we, their salvors, do not need and will not hold such property, and will assume no such ownership. Has not, therefore, all proprietary relation ceased?"

Historians writing about the Civil War sometimes use language that suggests emancipation was a gift bestowed by the North upon a passive slave population. This is a

OPPOSITE: **This photograph, taken in August or September 1863 near Culpeper, Virginia, shows two contrabands attached as laborers to the Army of the Potomac.**

flawed interpretation, because it fails to take into account the active role played by slaves in their own liberation. By acting on their own initiative, the runaways who sought refuge at Fortress Monroe pressured the Lincoln administration to address questions that it would much rather have ignored—such as the legal status of the runaways.

To declare the runaways free, as Butler seemed to be suggesting, was not yet a political possibility for Lincoln. To have done so would surely have offended the slave-holding border states of Kentucky, Missouri, Maryland, and Delaware, which Lincoln desperately needed to keep in the Union. On the other hand, if the "contrabands" (as the escaped slaves came to be called) were still property, to whom did they belong? For the time being, the best answer anyone could give was that they were the property of the U.S. government, although the government did little to exercise its ownership rights.

While in this legal limbo, some contrabands found work as laborers with the Union army. Others journeyed north, especially to Washington, D.C., where they were funneled into refugee camps. Elizabeth Keckley, Mary Lincoln's seamstress and confidant (and an African American herself), described their situation in her 1868 memoir:

> *Fresh from the bonds of slavery, fresh from the benighted regions of the plantation, they came to the Capital looking for liberty, and many of them not knowing it when they found it. Many good friends reached forth kind hands, but the North is not warm and impulsive. For one kind word spoken, two harsh ones were uttered; there was something repelling in the atmosphere, and the bright joyous dreams of freedom to the slave faded—were sadly altered, in the presence of that stern, practical mother, reality… Poor dusky children of slavery, men and women of my own race—the transition from slavery to freedom was too sudden for you! The bright dreams were too rudely dispelled; you were not prepared for the new life that opened before you, and the great masses of the North learned to look upon your helplessness with indifference—learned to speak of you as an idle, dependent race.*

In August 1861, Maj. Gen. John C. Frémont, commander of the Department of the West (mainly Missouri),

This Napoleonic portrait of Maj. Gen. George B. McClellan was produced by the Mathew Brady studio.

attempted to resolve the issue with an order freeing all Rebel-owned slaves within his department—a policy known as military emancipation. The order won the politically ambitious Frémont the acclaim of antislavery Republicans, who applauded his boldness; but it also raised the ire of his commander in chief, who feared the effect it would have on the loyalty of the border states (especially Kentucky). At first, Lincoln asked Frémont privately to rescind the emancipation order. When the egotistical general refused, Lincoln publicly ordered its retraction. "Genl. Frémont's proclamation, as to confiscation of property, and the liberation of slaves," the president wrote Orville Browning, "is purely political, and not within the range of military law, or necessity."

For a similar reason—that is, to curry favor with antislavery Republicans—Secretary of War Cameron endorsed the emancipation of contrabands in his annual report for 1861. In fact, Cameron went a good deal further than Frémont, proposing that the contrabands be armed so that they could fight for the Union. "It is as clearly a right of the Government," Cameron wrote, "to arm slaves, when it may become necessary, as it is to use gunpowder taken from the enemy." Bypassing the president, Cameron released his report to the press on December 1. Again, a displeased Lincoln walked the issue back, ordering the secretary to recall every copy of the report so that the offending sentences could be removed.

Thus, while the Army of the Potomac prepared for George McClellan's much-anticipated 1862 Peninsula Campaign against Richmond (the Confederate capital), the freedom of the contrabands remained unsettled—much

to the chagrin of Northern abolitionists. "To fight against slaveholders, without fighting against slavery, is but a half-hearted business, and paralyzes the hands engaged in it," Frederick Douglass complained. "War for the destruction of liberty must be met with war for the destruction of slavery."

Maj. Gen. David Hunter, one of the few abolitionists in the largely racist Union officer corps, agreed with Douglass. As commander of the Department of the South, Hunter controlled little territory—only the Union-occupied Sea Islands off the coasts of South Carolina and Georgia—but his nominal legal jurisdiction extended to the entirety of those states and Florida as well. Using this authority, on May 9, 1862, Hunter issued General Orders No. 11, which read:

An unidentified artist created this painting of George McClellan drilling his troops during the winter of 1861–62.

The three States of Georgia, Florida and South Carolina, comprising the Military Department of the South, having deliberately declared themselves no longer under the protection of the United States of America, and having taken up arms against the said United States, it becomes a military necessity to declare them under martial law; this was accordingly done on the 25th day of April, 1862.

Slavery and martial law in a free country are altogether incompatible; the persons in these three States, Georgia, Florida and South Carolina, heretofore held as slaves, are therefore, declared forever free.

Like Frémont's proclamation, Hunter's order ignored all three pillars of Lincoln's own emancipation strategy—gradualism, compensation, and colonization. Under Lincoln's plan, loyal slaveholders would relinquish their slaves gradually in exchange for federally provided compensation, with the understanding that the freed slaves would be encouraged to return to Africa or resettle elsewhere outside the United States. Although even Delaware, with its tiny slave population, repeatedly spurned the president's offer, Lincoln continued to make entreaties to the border states, believing that they would eventually have to accept the inevitability of emancipation and choose his method because it was the least disruptive. Such a political process would take time, however, during which Lincoln couldn't afford the interruption threatened by the introduction of military emancipation into the Department of the South.

Hunter's order certainly couldn't stand, but the president was never one to proceed heedlessly. True to his nature, he sought the counsel of several advisers, including that of Carl Schurz, his erstwhile ambassador to Spain, recently returned to the United States. If the president indeed overturned Hunter's order, Schurz recommended,

After Maj. Gen. David Hunter ordered the freeing of the slaves in his department, Lincoln complained privately, "I wanted him to do it, not say it."

he should be mindful that as Union armies occupied more and more Southern territory, "the force of circumstances will drive us into measures which were not in the original programme, but which necessity will oblige you to adopt.

"It seems to me of the greatest importance," Schurz continued, "that the government make no public declarations of policy which might be likely to embarrass it in the future. In fact you can hardly tell at the present moment how far you will have to go six weeks hence. The best policy would be to avoid public declarations altogether. The arming of negroes and the liberation of those slaves who offer us aid and assistance are things which must and will inevitably be done; in fact they are being done, and it would perhaps be best boldly to tell the whole truth and to acknowledge the necessity."

Lincoln knew that Schurz's analysis was correct, but he was not yet prepared to "tell the whole truth" because he didn't think the public was ready to hear it. He did, however, include in his May 19 revocation of Hunter's order a little-observed addendum reserving to himself alone the question of "whether it be competent for me, as Commander-in-Chief of the army and navy, to declare the slaves of any State or States free; and whether at any time, or in any case, it shall have become a necessity indispensable to the maintenance of the Government to exercise such supposed power."

EXACTLY when Lincoln changed his mind and decided to make emancipation a Union war aim is a matter of speculation and debate. According to the diary of Orville Browning, who was in Washington at the time representing Illinois in the Senate, Lincoln was working as late as July 1 on a cabinet document affirming his preference for gradual, compensated emancipation. Specifically, the document explained that while escaped Rebel-owned slaves would never be returned to their masters, whatever remained of slavery at the end of the Civil War would be left to the respective states to decide.

Three days later, on July 4, Charles Sumner of Massachusetts, the leading abolitionist in the Senate, urged Lincoln to celebrate the anniversary of the nation's independence by issuing a proclamation emancipating the slaves. Lincoln politely demurred. "I would do it," he told Sumner, "if I were not afraid that half the officers would fling down their arms and three more [border] States would rise."

Yet on July 13, Lincoln shared a startling confidence with Secretary of State Seward and Secretary of the Navy Gideon Welles. The occasion was a long carriage ride prompted by the recent death of Secretary of War Edwin Stanton's infant son. (Stanton had replaced the ineffective, likely corrupt Cameron in January 1862.) The carriage ride was long because the funeral was being held at the

Secretary of the Navy
Gideon Welles

house outside Georgetown where the Stantons were currently living. Like many highly placed residents of the capital (including the Lincolns), the Stantons habitually spent the summer months living in rented homes outside the city in order to escape Washington's brutal heat and humidity.

Along the way, Lincoln told Seward and Welles that he was seriously considering issuing a proclamation to emancipate the slaves. According to Welles' diary entry for that day, the president "dwelt earnestly on the gravity, importance, and delicacy of the movement, said he had given it much thought and had about come to the conclusion that it was a military necessity absolutely essential for the salvation of the Union, that we must free the slaves or be ourselves subdued." Then Lincoln asked his two cabinet colleagues for their frank opinions.

Seward was reluctant to answer, explaining that the consequences of emancipation were "so vast and momentous" that he needed some time to reflect on them before giving "a decisive answer." For the present, however, he did say that he was "inclined to the measure as justifiable, and perhaps . . . expedient and necessary." These were also Welles' views.

The proposal was, Welles continued, "a new departure for the President, for until that time, in all our previous interviews, whenever the question of emancipation or the mitigation of slavery had been in any way alluded to, he had been prompt and emphatic in denouncing any interference by the General Government with the subject."

As eventually drafted, the Emancipation Proclamation was indeed a stark departure from Lincoln's previous policy. It was not gradual, provided

Union troops use the Grapevine Bridge, constructed by the Fifth New Hampshire Infantry, to cross the Chickahominy River during the Peninsula Campaign.

no compensation, and did not mention colonization. Obviously, Lincoln's thinking had changed. Perhaps an epiphany did occur sometime between the president's exchange with Sumner on July 4 and the carriage ride on July 13; but it is much more likely that the transformation took place gradually over many months as military developments changed both the president's outlook and his perception of what the Northern public would accept. "I claim not to have controlled events," Lincoln would later write, "but confess plainly that events have controlled me."

Among the factors that most influenced Lincoln's change of mind were the utter failure of McClellan's Peninsula Campaign and other efforts to fight the war without targeting the Southern economy; the urgent need for additional military manpower; the renewed pressure for emancipation being applied by abolitionists in Congress; the border states' continuing rejection of gradual, compensated emancipation; and the "self-emancipation" being practiced by the slaves themselves, who continued to flock to Union lines. In addition, Lincoln knew from the extensive personal contacts he maintained outside Washington that Northern attitudes concerning slavery had shifted considerably since the beginning of the war.

For more than a year now, Union soldiers had been force-fed an up-close view of slavery, and they wrote home regularly to describe what they saw. "Since I am here," a Democratic colonel wrote from Louisiana in one such letter, "I have learned and seen . . . what the horror of slavery was . . . Never hereafter will I either speak or vote in favor of slavery." Future president James A. Garfield similarly observed in a letter to his family in Ohio that "the rank and file of the army [are] steadily and surely becoming imbued with sympathy for the slaves and hatred for slavery." These and thousands of other letters helped reverse a great deal of thoughtless, complacent racism; and the military stalemate likewise encouraged Northerners to accept the idea that emancipated Southern slaves could bolster the Union war effort.

"All his life, Lincoln had exhibited an exceptionally sensitive grasp of the limits set by public opinion," Doris Kearns Goodwin has written. "As a politician, he had an intuitive sense of when to hold fast, when to wait, and when to lead." Lincoln's sense now told him that the time to lead on emancipation had finally arrived.

Before the Confederate victory at the first battle of Bull Run, while Northerners still believed that the South could be defeated quickly and decisively, it seemed prudent to limit Union war aims to restoration of the status quo ante bellum without taking on the difficult question of slavery (beyond halting its expansion to the western territories). But as the war lengthened and the casualties mounted, the enormous expenditures of blood and treasure persuaded many Northerners to accept the abolitionists' contention that the preservation of the Union required the emancipation of the slaves, if only because the slaves were an important military and economic resource.

Lincoln's moment of decision, Eric Foner has suggested, may have come on July 7, when the president traveled to Harrison's Landing on the James River to meet with General McClellan, who had just been whipped by

> MANY of my strongest supporters urged emancipation before I thought it indispensable, and, I may say, before I thought the country ready for it. It is my conviction that, had the proclamation been issued even six months earlier than it was, public sentiment would not have sustained it. Just so, as to the subsequent action in reference to enlisting blacks in the Border States. The step, taken sooner, could not, in my judgment, have been carried out. A man watches his pear tree day after day, impatient for the ripening of the fruit. Let him attempt to *force* the process, and he may spoil both fruit and tree. But let him patiently wait, and the ripe pear at length falls into his lap! We have seen this great revolution in public sentiment slowly but *surely* progressing, so that, when final action came, the opposition was not strong enough to defeat the purpose.
>
> **—ABRAHAM LINCOLN**
> (In conversation with British antislavery activist
> George Thompson, April 17, 1864)

This anti-McClellan cartoon shows the general watching the July 1, 1862, battle of Malvern Hill from the safety of a gunboat in the James River. His absence from the battlefield led some to charge him with the cowardice shown here.

Robert E. Lee in the Seven Days' Battles. At this meeting, the still-arrogant McClellan handed Lincoln a letter demanding that the war be conducted "upon the highest principles known to Christian Civilization." Neither the confiscation of property nor the "forcible abolition of slavery should be contemplated for a moment," McClellan wrote. Ironically, the letter seems to have led Lincoln to the opposite conclusion. According to Foner, "He departed convinced that the war could not possibly be won in this manner, and that what would come to be called 'hard war'—war not simply of army against army but of society against society—had become necessary." No longer, in other words, could Southern civilians be shielded from the consequences of secession.

Lincoln returned to Washington on July 10. Two days later, he met with a delegation of congressmen from the border states and pressed them once again to accept gradual, compensated emancipation. Again they refused. The next day, July 13, he rode to Georgetown with Seward and Welles.

LINCOLN met with his cabinet on Tuesdays and Fridays. At a special meeting on Monday, July 21, he read several draft orders, which the cabinet approved unanimously. The most significant of these was an order authorizing Union armies in hostile territory to live off the land by appropriating civilian property as needed. The cabinet also took up the matter of General Hunter's

Contrabands employed by the
U.S. Army Quartermaster in
Alexandria, Virginia.

W HEN, early in the war, Gen. Frémont attempted military emancipation, I forbade it, because I did not then think it an indispensable necessity. When a little later, Gen. Cameron, then Secretary of War, suggested the arming of the blacks, I objected, because I did not yet think it an indispensable necessity. When, still later, Gen. Hunter attempted military emancipation, I again forbade it, because I did not yet think the indispensable necessity had come. When, in March, and May, and July 1862 I made earnest, and successive appeals to the border states to favor compensated emancipation, I believed the indispensable necessity for military emancipation, and arming the blacks would come, unless averted by that measure. They declined the proposition; and I was, in my best judgment, driven to the alternative of either surrendering the Union, and with it, the Constitution, or of laying strong hand upon the colored element. I chose the latter.

—ABRAHAM LINCOLN
(Comments to members of a
Kentucky delegation, March 26, 1864)

request that he be permitted to enlist Negro soldiers. No conclusion was reached, so the cabinet reconvened on Tuesday, July 22, to continue its discussion.

Seward and Welles were less surprised than the others when Lincoln read a new order that he had drafted during the night. It consisted of three parts. The first warned Southerners to end their rebellion or suffer the confiscation of their property, including their slaves. The second offered complying Rebels financial compensation for the gradual emancipation of their slaves. The third, which specifically invoked Lincoln's authority as commander in chief, declared that on January 1, 1863, "all persons held as slaves within any state or states, wherein the constitutional authority of the United States shall not then be practically recognized, submitted to, and maintained, shall then, thenceforward, and forever, be free." This awkwardly phrased order, presented without fanfare, was the first draft of the Emancipation Proclamation.

Until July 22, Lincoln had consistently blocked or revoked every effort to overturn the institution of slavery lest the border states take umbrage and secede. Yet now the only concession he made to these states was to exempt their territory from the order (because they "recognized, submitted to, and maintained" the Constitution). Similarly, until July 22, Lincoln had carefully distinguished between loyal and disloyal slaveholders, always respecting the rights of the former. Now, he made no such distinction. Finally, until July 22, Lincoln had been cautious not to exceed the powers granted him under the Constitution. Now, he asserted boldly that he had the authority as commander in chief to emancipate immediately and irrevocably millions of slaves without providing any compensation to their owners.

The cabinet secretaries didn't know how to react. Most were stunned into silence; and even those who weren't shocked needed time to take in the magnitude of what Lincoln had just said. As Welles later wrote, the president's proposal was "fraught with consequences, immediate and remote, such as human foresight could not penetrate." Would the proclamation stiffen the resolve of the South? Would it divide the North? No one knew for certain; all they could do was speculate.

Of those who expressed reservations, the most vocal was conservative Postmaster General Montgomery Blair, who worried that a general emancipation order would hurt Republican candidates in the fall, when the congressional midterm elections would be held. Only William Seward, whom Lincoln had given nine days' notice, had a more considered opinion to offer.

As secretary of state, Seward had been receiving for several months reports from concerned diplomats overseas. These ambassadors were worried that the Union's lack of military progress might embolden foreign governments (especially those interested in obtaining Southern cotton) to recognize the Confederacy as an independent nation. The way to forestall such an unfortunate development, they recommended, was to make emancipation an explicit Union war aim. Even Great Britain, which craved Southern cotton for its bustling textile mills, would be far less likely to intervene on behalf of the Confederacy if the issue were the South's right to practice slavery rather than simply its right to self-determination.

Based on this logic, one might reasonably conclude that a presidential emancipation order would stop at once all such movement toward Confederate recognition. Yet Seward saw that issuing such an order in the immediate aftermath of McClellan's defeat would likely have the opposite effect. Given the Union army's woeful

After meeting New York artist Francis B. Carpenter, Lincoln encouraged him to paint *First Reading of the Emancipation Proclamation of President Lincoln* (1864) by allowing him to live in the White House for six months.

performance in the Peninsula Campaign, the president's order would seem to be an act of desperation and thus signal weakness. Far better, Seward said, for the president to postpone issuing the order until a military victory could be achieved. Lincoln thought carefully about what Seward had to say; and in the end, he took the secretary's advice.

It was during this waiting period suggested by Seward that Horace Greeley published his "Prayer of Twenty Millions." Given that Lincoln had already decided privately to make emancipation a war aim, his response to Greeley seems somewhat disingenuous to modern readers. But Lincoln's purpose in making a public reply wasn't simply to conceal. Rather, he used the reply as an opportunity to help prepare the public for the argument that was to come: that the survival of the Union depended on the emancipation of the Southern slaves. Certainly,

the president had a keen grasp of the limits set by public opinion; but he also had a remarkable ability to shape that opinion with his carefully conceived public utterances. "His speeches and writing, plain, homely, and unpublished as they sometime are," Illinois congressman Isaac N. Arnold observed, "have become the household words of the people, and crystallized into the overwhelming public sentiment which demands the extinction of slavery."

For two months after the July 22 cabinet meeting, the war continued to go poorly for the Union, and Lincoln continued to wait. McClellan's failure to reposition the Army of the Potomac quickly enough to reinforce John Pope's Army of Virginia—deliberately, Secretary of War Stanton believed, to make the newly appointed Pope look bad—led in late August to another debacle at the second battle of Bull Run, the dismissal of Pope, and the reappointment

This 1888 Kurz & Allison lithograph celebrates the fight at Burnside Bridge during the battle of Antietam.

of McClellan. Pressing his advantage, Lee moved north across the Potomac, invading Maryland on September 4. Rumors swept Washington that the city was about to be overrun. In fact, Lee had no plans to attack the capital, which had become one of the most heavily fortified cities in the world. Instead, he planned to send two-thirds of the Army of Northern Virginia (under the command of Maj. Gen. Thomas J. "Stonewall" Jackson) to capture Harpers Ferry, West Virginia, while keeping the remaining third under his own command in Maryland.

Dividing one's forces in hostile territory is always risky; but, as James M. McPherson has noted, "Two of Lee's hallmarks as a commander were his ability to judge an opponent's qualities and his willingness to take risks." In this case, given McClellan's overly cautious nature, Lee judged that the risks were justified. "His army is in a very demoralized and chaotic condition," Lee remarked to a subordinate at the time, "and will not be prepared for offensive operations—or he will not think it so—for three or four weeks. Before that time, I hope to be on the Susquehanna."

Lee would likely have made it to Pennsylvania in the fall of 1862 had not two roving Union soldiers discovered by chance a mislaid copy of Lee's orders to Jackson. "Now I know what to do!" McClellan exclaimed upon reading

Dead soldiers litter the ground in front of the Dunker Church, the focal point of several Union assaults against the Confederate left flank during the battle of Antietam.

the orders. To be sure, the Union commander continued to delay; but he did move faster than he would have otherwise—and certainly faster than Lee had anticipated. Hurrying back from Harpers Ferry, Jackson arrived just in time to avert disaster but not soon enough to save the day for the Confederates. In all, six thousand Americans died and another eighteen thousand were wounded at the battle of Antietam, fought on September 17, the single bloodiest day in American history. On the night of September 18–19, the exhausted Army of Northern Virginia retreated back across the Potomac, its advance halted.

Although Lincoln understood that McClellan's characteristic lack of aggressiveness had cost the Union forces a rare opportunity to smash Lee's divided army and perhaps move on to Richmond, he chose to embrace the general's "victory" nonetheless because it offered him the political opportunity he needed to issue his emancipation order. To that end, five days after the battle, he signed the Preliminary Emancipation Proclamation. Its content and structure were essentially unchanged from the July 22 draft, but its argument was more elaborate and its language more polished.

WHEN the rebel army was at Frederick, I determined, as soon as it should be driven out of Maryland, to issue a Proclamation of Emancipation such as I thought most likely to be useful. I said nothing to any one; but I made the promise to myself, and (hesitating a little) to my Maker. The rebel army is now driven out, and I am going to fulfill that promise. I have got you together to hear what I have written down. I do not wish your advice about the main matter—for that I have determined for myself. This I say without intending any thing but respect for any one of you. But I already know the views of each on this question. They have been heretofore expressed, and I have considered them as thoroughly and carefully as I can. What I have written is that which my reflections have determined me to say.

—ABRAHAM LINCOLN
(As recorded in Salmon P. Chase's diary, September 22, 1862)

EVEN though many in Washington had been expecting some sort of presidential emancipation order, its publication on September 23 still drew a strong reaction. Congressmen from the border states expressed their vehement opposition, but Lincoln was cheered by the large crowd that gathered outside the White House. "I can only trust in God I have made no mistake," the president proclaimed from an upstairs window in response to the crowd's applause. "I shall make no attempt on this occasion to sustain what I have done or said by any comment. It is now for the country and the world to pass judgment on it."

The initial judgment was not positive. In the 1862 midterm elections, the president's party fared poorly, with the Democrats gaining thirty-two seats in the House. Although the Republicans did hold enough seats to control the new Thirty-eighth Congress, their majority had slipped badly, justifying Blair's concerns and auguring ill for the national party's prospects in 1864. Even so, Lincoln, having come deliberately to his decision, remained committed to the new emancipation policy.

Although the president didn't really expect any Rebels to heed his warning, he did wait until January 1, 1863, before issuing the final order. He had planned to sign the formal document before attending the annual White House New Year's Day reception, which began at eleven o'clock. But upon reviewing the document, he noticed that it had a slight technical error requiring correction by the State Department. While Seward attended to this, Lincoln spent the next three hours shaking hands with the public before returning to his office about two o'clock.

With Seward by his side, he sat down at his desk and picked up a pen—only to put it down again when he saw that his hand was trembling. The cause wasn't nervousness, he explained, but fatigue after so much handshaking. "I do not want it to appear as if I hesitated," he said, so he paused a few moments while the trembling subsided. Ever aware of the historical significance of his actions, Lincoln knew that this act would be especially well remembered. So instead of using the simple "A. Lincoln" signature that he typically affixed to government

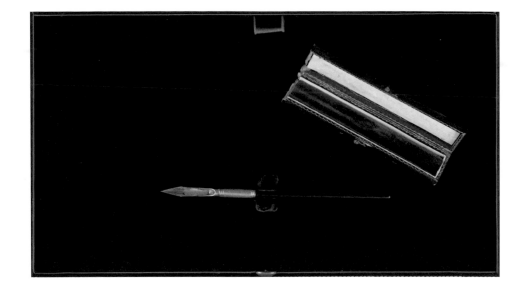

The gold pen used by President Lincoln on January 1, 1863, to sign the Final Emancipation Proclamation.

documents, he signed this one with his full name.

Because the Final Emancipation Proclamation included exemptions for the loyal border states, Union-occupied Tennessee, and Union-held areas in Louisiana and Virginia, some abolitionists charged that the order freed no slaves at all, because the three million men, women, and children to whom it did apply remained in Rebel hands beyond the order's practical reach. This criticism was not entirely correct. Neither the Sea Islands nor Union-controlled territory in Arkansas, Florida, Mississippi, and North Carolina was included in the exemptions; thus, the president's order immediately freed about fifty thousand slaves.

But such arguments miss the point of the order. As Frederick Douglass realized, the most important aspect of the Emancipation Proclamation was its guarantee of freedom to any slave who chose to leave his Rebel master for the Union lines. This was an irresistible enticement; and in the turbulence of war, with so many women minding plantations in the absence of their soldier husbands, slaves had ample opportunity to escape. But the Union armies would have to move close enough to make such a leap of

MY own opinion of the history of the emancipation proclamation is, that Mr. Lincoln foresaw the necessity for it—long before he issued it—He was anxious to avoid it—and came to it only when he saw that the measure would subtract from their [the Southerners'] labor [force] and add to our army quite a number of good fighting men . . .

I remember well our conversation on the subject—He seemed to treat it as certain that I would recognize the wisdom of the act when I should see the harvest of good which we would erelong glean from it—In that conversation he alluded to an incident in his life, long passed, when he was so much depressed that he almost contemplated suicide—At the time of his deep depression—He said to me that he had done nothing to make any human being remember that he had lived—and that to connect his name with the events transpiring in his day & generation and so impress himself upon them as to link his name with something that would redound to the interest of his fellow man was what he desired to live for—He reminded me of the conversation—and said with earnest emphasis—I believe that in this measure (meaning his proclamation) my fondest hopes will be realized.

—JOSHUA SPEED
(Letter to William H. Herndon, February 7, 1866)

faith possible. In this way, emancipation became inextricably yoked to Union military success. The former could not proceed without the latter.

BECAUSE the avowed purpose of the Emancipation Proclamation was to strengthen the Union war effort, it included this sentence: "And I further declare and make known that such persons of suitable condition will be received into the armed service of the United States to garrison forts, positions, stations, and other places, and to

man vessels of all sorts in said service." In other words, the president was granting his field commanders permission to recruit African Americans into the Union army and navy.

Even those officers and soldiers averse to serving with Negroes—and there were many—recognized the logic of the president's reasoning. Two years into the war, the Army of the Potomac was no closer to Richmond than it had been at the war's outset. More extreme measures were plainly required; and Lincoln, having deliberated long enough, now moved forward with clear-eyed resolve. "The colored population is the great available and yet unavailed of, force for restoring the Union," he wrote in March 1863 to Andrew Johnson, the military governor of Tennessee. "The bare sight of fifty thousand armed and drilled black soldiers on the banks of the Mississippi would end the rebellion at once. And who doubts that we can present that sight if we but take hold in earnest? If you have been thinking of it please do not dismiss the thought."

Initially, it was the expectation of Lincoln and others in the government that black soldiers would perform manual labor and other mundane tasks—digging trenches, serving as cooks, and so on—thereby freeing additional white soldiers for combat duty. Consequently (and no doubt because of unconscious racism as well), Congress established a reduced pay scale for black troops. At a time when

White officers and black laborers of the Second Rhode Island Volunteer Infantry at Camp Brightwood, D.C.

white soldiers were paid thirteen dollars a month, black soldiers received only ten dollars per month, less a three-dollar-per-month clothing deduction that white soldiers didn't have to pay.

Another factor was that most whites, including Lincoln, weren't sure that black soldiers could or would fight. "If we were to arm them," the president wrote in September 1862, "I fear that in a few weeks the arms would be in the hands of the rebels." Some of his constituents feared even worse: that armed Negroes would turn their guns indiscriminately on whites, Northerners and Southerners alike.

Whatever temptations former slaves might have felt, those who fled their masters to join the Union army in 1863 served with such distinction that their behavior forced another dramatic shift in Northern public opinion. Once again, thousands of erstwhile slaves—this time aided by some free Northern brethren—played a crucial role in achieving their own liberation. Of particular importance were three battles fought in the late spring and early summer of 1863.

On May 27, a large Union force under Maj. Gen. Nathaniel P. Banks attacked the Rebel stronghold of Port

The Fifty-fourth Massachusetts Volunteer Infantry attacks Fort Wagner in this 1890 Kurz & Allison lithograph.

Hudson, Louisiana, on the Mississippi River. Because of the widespread prejudice against Negro troops, neither of the two black regiments attached to Banks—the First and Third Louisiana Native Guards—was assigned to take part in the assault. However, when firm Confederate resistance halted the Union advance, Brig. Gen. William Dwight, Jr., ordered the Native Guards forward into the attack. Port Hudson held, but the spirited performance of the black soldiers made a lasting impression on their white commanders. "The severe test to which they were subjected, and the determined manner in which they encountered the enemy," Banks wrote in his official report, "leaves upon my mind no doubt of their ultimate success."

About a week later, on June 7, Confederate troops attempted to break the Union siege of Vicksburg by attacking Maj. Gen. Ulysses S. Grant's supply depot at Milliken's Bend. There followed a fierce, close-quarters battle during which the depot's primarily black garrison drove off the Rebels. According to Assistant Secretary of War Charles A. Dana, who was with Grant's army at the time, "The bravery of the blacks completely revolutionized the sentiment of the army with regard to the employment of negro troops."

Yet neither Port Hudson nor Milliken's Bend matched the battle of Fort Wagner for its impact on Northern public opinion. A strategic Confederate battery on Morris Island, Fort Wagner guarded the entrance to Charleston Harbor. Its reduction would strengthen the Union naval blockade and cut South Carolina off from the rest of the world. The attack took place on July 18, led by the Fifty-fourth Massachusetts Volunteer Infantry, the most publicized Negro regiment because it came from an abolitionist state and contained so many free Northern blacks. Sadly, the assault against Fort Wagner was ill conceived. The only approach to the fort lay along a narrow stretch of beach, which quickly became a killing ground. Of the six hundred men in the regiment, nearly

A black soldier from Maryland posed for this ambrotype with his wife and daughters.
To encourage the enlistment of border-state slaves in the Union army, Congress extended
emancipation in 1865 to the families of volunteers as well.

half were killed or wounded. Even so, the soldiers kept fighting until their white officers finally ordered a retreat. Their courage and sacrifice proved beyond any doubt that African Americans would fight.

Three weeks later, Lincoln wrote to Grant advising him that "at least a hundred thousand [black troops] can, and ought to be rapidly organized." Such troops, the president continued, constituted "a resource which, if vigorously applied now, will soon close the contest. It works doubly, weakening the enemy and strengthening us." Although two of Grant's officers resigned rather than accept black troops, the general himself agreed with

Lincoln's appraisal. "I have given the subject of arming the Negro my hearty support," Grant replied. "This, with the emancipation of the Negro, is the heaviest blow yet given the Confederacy."

Of course, using Negroes as soldiers inevitably raised the issue of what would become of the black veterans when the war was over. At least this was certain: they wouldn't be colonized. "It would hardly be treating the African like a man," one Maryland newspaperman observed, "to use him as a soldier and then banish him."

III

A Singular Nation

ALTHOUGH race baiting had carried many Democrats to victory in 1862, attacks on Lincoln's "nigger sympathies" became much less effective once the worth of the black soldiers became apparent. In fact, no doubt influenced by the shifting public mood, a number of influential War Democrats turned against slavery in 1863—some because they recognized the military benefits (if not the morality) of emancipation; others because they could see the increasing harm that opposition to emancipation was doing to their party.

Understanding the political importance of these Democrats, not only to his reelection but also to the passage of future Reconstruction legislation, Lincoln courted them throughout 1863 and 1864. He was aided in this effort by Seward; Montgomery Blair; and Montgomery's father, Francis Preston Blair, Sr.

Among the nation's most influential political families, the Blairs were lapsed Democrats who maintained extensive contacts with members of their former party. Francis Preston Blair had been one of Andrew Jackson's closest advisers—a member of Old Hickory's Kitchen Cabinet and editor of the *Washington Globe*, the Democratic party's principal organ in the nation's capital. After Jackson's death, the elder Blair separated from the party's mainstream, becoming a Free Soiler and later one of the founders of the Republican party. Lincoln appointed Francis' eldest son, Montgomery, to be postmaster general so that the Republican party's conservative wing, which the Blairs represented, could have a seat in the president's cabinet. For all the Blairs' usefulness, however, they could also be

This 1863 *Harper's Weekly* cartoon shows Copperheads advancing on Columbia, the personification of the Union.

troublesome because they were deeply racist, often attacking members of the party's abolitionist wing (known as Radical Republicans) for their support of racial equality before the law.

In general, the president's effort to build a governing coalition of centrist Republicans and pro-emancipation Democrats fared well. In the fall 1863 gubernatorial elections, coalition candidates turned back strong challenges from Copperheads in Ohio and Pennsylvania. For this reason, Lincoln was in a rather good mood when he boarded a train for southern Pennsylvania on November 18.

The president was traveling to Pennsylvania because he had been invited to attend the dedication of a new national cemetery in Gettysburg, established to reinter the remains of Union soldiers who had died there four months earlier. Former Harvard University president

OPPOSITE: **Mathew Brady photographed this view along Washington's South B Street (now Independence Avenue) in 1863. On the left is the Smithsonian Institution.**

A view of the crowd at the dedication of the Gettysburg cemetery where Lincoln delivered his famously brief address.

Edward Everett was scheduled to be the principal speaker, but Lincoln understood that he would be expected to say a few words.

Everett's memorized speech, which lasted two hours, presented a detailed history of the murderous three-day battle, punctuated with erudite references to classical antiquity and political philosophy. Following a musical interlude, the president was introduced. His speech was brief, just ten sentences long. The next day, Everett wrote to Lincoln, "I should be glad, if I could flatter myself that I came as near to the central idea of the occasion, in two hours, as you did in two minutes."

To grasp the full meaning of what the president had to say, one must recall that in 1863, the era of the American Revolution was not yet the distant past it is today. To modern ears, "four score and seven years" evokes an almost biblical time. But to Americans of Lincoln's generation, whose grandparents fought in the Revolutionary War, the creation of the United States was not so remote a collective memory. Moreover, in the eighty-seven years that had passed since the Declaration of Independence, no other nation had yet followed the same self-governing path. For Lincoln and his contemporaries, the success of the American experiment in self-government remained an open question; and during the Civil War, in particular, Lincoln feared that he might be presiding over its failure.

As Horace Greeley had pointed out in December 1860 during the first days of the secession crisis, "We hold the right of Self-Government sacred, even when invoked in behalf of those who deny it to others." Yet so much had transpired during the intervening three years that in 1863, neither Greeley nor his readership conceived of self-government in quite the same way.

Before the Civil War, Americans used *United States* primarily as a plural noun. That is, people would say, "The

United States are in North America." During the war, however, usage changed, and Northerners began referring to *United States* in the singular, emphasizing its unity—as in "The United States is a proud nation." Similarly, the word *nation* came to replace *Union* as the most common synonym for the country. In his first inaugural address, Lincoln used the word *Union* nineteen times and *nation* not once. In the Gettysburg Address, he used *nation* five times and *Union* not once.

These changes in usage reflected changes in how Americans, at least in the North, viewed their country. In 1782, at the suggestion of Thomas Jefferson, the Continental Congress had placed the phrase *E pluribus unum* on the Great Seal of the United States. This Latin motto, borrowed from Virgil's poem *Moretum*, means "out of many, one." Yet Americans didn't truly conceive of themselves as a single people until the outbreak of the Civil War made them think long and hard about what it meant to be an American.

It was principally this new sense of nationhood that the president was affirming in his Gettysburg Address. But Lincoln also wanted to make it plain that the postwar, singular United States would have to honor much more faithfully Jefferson's proposition that "all men are created equal." The president's audience, both at Gettysburg and in the nation at large, certainly understood that by "new birth of freedom," Lincoln meant that the slaves who had been emancipated could never be returned to bondage—at least not while he was president.

THE battle of Gettysburg—fought on July 1–3, 1863—had been an important victory for the Union army, halting Lee's second (and much more aggressive) invasion of the North. So, too, had been the July 4 reduction of Vicksburg, giving the Federals navigational control of the Mississippi River and cutting the Confederacy in half. But the war was far from over, and there were many challenges ahead, notably the rout of the Army of the Cumberland at Chickamauga in September 1863 (leading to the besiegement of Union forces in Chattanooga) and the relentless stalemate along the eastern front.

Because Maj. Gen. George G. Meade, the hero of Gettysburg, was unable to move the Army of the Potomac any closer to Richmond, Lincoln made another command change during the winter of 1863–64. On March 9, he promoted Ulysses S. Grant to lieutenant general and three

FOUR score and seven years ago our fathers brought forth on this continent a new nation, conceived in liberty, and dedicated to the proposition that all men are created equal.

Now we are engaged in a great civil war, testing whether that nation, or any nation so conceived and so dedicated, can long endure. We are met on a great battlefield of that war. We have come to dedicate a portion of that field as a final resting-place for those who here gave their lives that the nation might live. It is altogether fitting and proper that we should do this.

But, in a larger sense, we cannot dedicate, we cannot consecrate, we cannot hallow, this ground. The brave men, living and dead, who struggled here have consecrated it, far above our poor power to add or detract. The world will little note, nor long remember, what we say here, but it can never forget what they did here. It is for us the living, rather, to be dedicated here to the unfinished work which they who fought here have thus far so nobly advanced. It is rather for us to be here dedicated to the great task remaining before us—that from these honored dead we take increased devotion to that cause for which they gave the last full measure of devotion— that we here highly resolve that these dead shall not have died in vain—that this nation, under God, shall have a new birth of freedom and that government of the people, by the people, for the people, shall not perish from the earth.

—**ABRAHAM LINCOLN**
(Gettysburg Address, November 19, 1863)

Maj. Gen. Ulysses S. Grant (lower left) on Lookout Mountain. Grant's victories there and on Missionary Ridge chased Braxton Bragg's Rebels into Georgia, setting the stage for Maj. Gen. William T. Sherman's Atlanta campaign.

days later gave him command of all Union armies. Lincoln had been watching Grant for some time. When a friend insisted to the president that Grant be removed from his field command after the disaster at Shiloh in April 1862, Lincoln refused, saying, "I can't spare this man; he fights." A year later, after Grant's triumph at Vicksburg, Lincoln told a confidant, "Grant is my man, and I am his, for the rest of the war." When Grant broke the siege of Chattanooga and chased the Confederates from Lookout Mountain and Missionary Ridge in November 1863, the president knew it was finally time to bring the general east.

A self-effacing man of action with little concern for his public image (or his personal appearance), Grant proved to be the opposite of McClellan in nearly every way, much to Lincoln's satisfaction. On the other hand, the public view of Grant was more conflicted. The president wanted aggressiveness, and he got it; but the consequences of that aggression, if necessary, were difficult for many Northerners to accept.

In May 1864, when the spring rains finally subsided, making the Virginia roads passable, Grant ordered the Army of the Potomac to cross the Rapidan River and move around Lee's right flank toward the Confederate capital. With 122,000 men, Grant had nearly twice the numerical strength of Lee's 66,000-man Army of Northern Virginia; but the densely forested terrain through which the Federals had to pass (known as the Wilderness) acted as a force equalizer. During the two-day battle of the Wilderness that began on May 5, the Federals lost 17,000 men, compared to perhaps 11,000 casualties for the Rebels.

Bloodied in this way, past Union commanders had chosen to retreat, but Grant was different. He agonized over the losses, often turning to liquor for solace, but he never pulled back. "That man," Confederate lieutenant general James Longstreet warned presciently, "will fight us every day and every hour till the end of the war." Indeed, as Longstreet realized, Grant's goal was brutally single-minded: not so much the capture of Richmond as the destruction of Lee's army.

Beginning on May 8, the two hosts met again at Spotsylvania Court House, and again the bloodshed was shocking. Grant lost another eighteen thousand men; Lee, significantly less but still a great many. (The exact Southern casualties are unknown because Confederate record keeping, never very good, deteriorated during the last years of the war.) Given these results, one might consider the battle a victory for the Rebels, but both Grant and Lee knew better. While Grant had ready access to reinforcements,

Lee did not, making attrition a very serious threat to the Rebel army's survival.

At dawn on June 3, Grant struck Lee again at Cold Harbor. The assault was ill advised, because Lee's position (which Grant's staff had failed to inspect carefully) was especially well fortified. During the main charge, which lasted only ten minutes, seven thousand Northern soldiers were killed, wounded, captured, or went missing— compared to about fifteen hundred Southerners. It was Grant's worst defeat of the war; but despite the horrific loss of life, he kept pushing forward. Nine days later, Grant began moving elements of his army toward the James River, where they would join Benjamin Butler's Army of the James on June 15 for a surprise attack against Petersburg, a strategic rail junction located about twenty miles south of Richmond.

Although Petersburg guarded the southern approach to the Confederate capital, it was only lightly defended at the time by a three-thousand-man garrison under P. G. T. Beauregard. In all likelihood, Petersburg would have fallen to Butler's sixteen thousand Federals that day had it not been for a combination of timidity and tardiness on Butler's part that gave Beauregard the time he needed to reinforce his position. With Butler's way now blocked, the arriving Army of the Potomac had no route to the capital; and so Grant's forces piled up on one side

LEFT: A Union burial party gathers remains on the Cold Harbor battlefield.

BELOW: The instrument case of a Union army surgeon. Antiseptic surgery was still years away.

Members of the Third Massachusetts Heavy Artillery man a hundred-pound Parrott gun at Fort Totten on the outskirts of Washington.

AS Northern morale sank to its lowest point of the war, calls for peace grew louder once again. "Stop the War!" headlined one Democratic editorial. "If nothing else would impress upon the people the absolute necessity of stopping this war, its utter failure to accomplish any results would be sufficient."

In early June, the Republican party (now calling itself the National Union party to accommodate Democratic coalition members) had renominated Lincoln overwhelmingly, adding War Democrat Andrew Johnson to the ticket as vice president. But as the summer months passed and the military situation worsened, the president's popularity fell so precipitously that many Republicans began calling for him to step down in favor of a less damaged candidate. The still-influential Horace Greeley wrote to Lincoln that "our bleeding, bankrupt, almost dying country . . . shudders at the prospect of fresh conscriptions, of further wholesale devastations, and of new rivers of human blood." Given the despondent mood of the country, even close friends of the president such as Illinois lawyer Leonard Swett came to doubt his electability. "Unless material changes can be wrought," Swett wrote to his wife, "Lincoln's election is beyond any possible hope."

The president's political standing was further undermined by infighting between the party's conservative and Radical wings. In February and again in May, Montgomery Blair's younger brother Frank, a Missouri congressman, speaking on the floor of the House, savaged Secretary of the Treasury Chase while lashing out at Chase's Radical colleagues for their support of emancipation. The president's failure to defend Chase and disavow Blair's racist screeds angered many Radicals, who broke from the party in May to nominate John C. Frémont on an independent ticket.

The split became even wider when Lincoln pocket-vetoed the Wade-Davis Bill on July 4, the last day of the Thirty-eighth Congress' first session. Named for its sponsors, Sen. Benjamin F. "Bluff" Wade of Ohio and Rep. Henry Winter Davis of Maryland, the bill established rigorous conditions for the readmission of Confederate states to the Union. It was based on Charles Sumner's "state suicide" theory, which held that secession amounted

of the front while Lee raced to the other. As at Vicksburg, Grant experimented with a few frontal assaults, but these proved worthless; and so, beginning on June 18, the two sides settled down into a prolonged siege.

On the war's other fronts, the news was no better. In the trans-Mississippi West, Nathaniel Banks failed in his spring 1864 effort to capture Louisiana's Red River Valley; and Maj. Gen. William T. Sherman, having left Chattanooga for Atlanta, was making but slow headway against Gen. Joseph E. Johnston's Army of Tennessee. When a Confederate corps under Lt. Gen. Jubal A. Early crossed the Potomac and defeated a Union force at the Monocacy River on July 9, the dejection turned to panic. Two days later, when Early's army arrived in Silver Spring on the outskirts of Washington, anxious Union commanders ordered soldiers convalescing in the capital's many army hospitals to leave their beds and reinforce the city's defenses. (The arrival of two Union corps from Petersburg stabilized the situation, prompting Early's withdrawal.)

By July 19, when Lincoln called for another five hundred thousand troops, few Northerners believed their side was winning the war—and if that was so, why continue the astonishing bloodshed?

to an "abdication by the State of all rights under the Constitution." Once a state lost its legitimacy in this way, according to Sumner, it reverted to the status of a territory, which Congress was entitled to govern as it saw fit.

Among the conditions for readmission set by the Wade-Davis Bill was a requirement that a majority of a state's 1860 voting population swear a loyalty oath to the Constitution. (The president's plan, in comparison, required only 10 percent of the 1860 voting population to swear a lesser oath.) The Rebel states would also have to abolish slavery before they could be readmitted.

Lincoln decided to veto the bill because he refused to accept the state-suicide theory. Specifically, he believed that Sumner's theory recognized the departure of the Confederate states from the Union. Therefore, if he signed the bill, he would be legitimizing secession. The Wade-Davis legislation, he told Zachariah Chandler, a Radical senator from Michigan, "seems to me to make the fatal admission that States whenever they please may of their own motion dissolve their connection with the Union. Now we cannot survive that admission, I am convinced. If that be true, I am not President; these gentlemen are not Congress."

On August 5, Wade and Davis responded

CAN it be that Mr. Lincoln is going to continue in being controlled, as he has been, in his policy by the Blairs? If Mr. Lincoln is not willing to put himself in a position and insist with all the power of the whole Government to effectually make every State free during his four new years he is looking forward to, there are a very large class of earnest men who will feel very little interest in this contest. Is it not possible to make Mr. Lincoln comprehend this? Or are we to go through with this election and have four years more of procrastination and then die broken hearted at having failed in our only chance, because we had a President who says he wants to make all free, but is too big a coward.

—JOHN HIESTAND
(Pennsylvania journalist's letter to
Rep. Thaddeus Stevens, May 29, 1864)

BELOW LEFT: "When This Cruel War Is Over" was the best-selling song of 1864, reflecting the low Northern morale.

BELOW: After three years of war, images such as this one—of the first day's dead at Gettysburg—gave Northerners pause to consider the accumulated loss of life.

publicly with an attack on Lincoln in Greeley's *New York Tribune*. Meanwhile, other calumnies piled on. Radicals complained that the president was a dawdling Southern sympathizer; Democrats labeled him a dictator for using his war powers to suspend the writ of habeas corpus and close down inflammatory opposition newspapers. To most observers, the political situation seemed hopeless; and on August 22, the Republican National Committee, meeting in New York, concluded that, as matters stood, Lincoln could not be reelected. Chairman Henry J. Raymond, the owner and editor of the *New York Times*, was delegated to deliver the bad news. In a letter posted that day, Raymond passed on both the committee's conclusion and what it believed to be Lincoln's only way out. The president, Raymond advised, should immediately dispatch an envoy to Richmond with an offer of peace based on the sole condition of reunion.

One can infer that Raymond's letter distressed Lincoln because of what happened next: on the morning of August 23, the letter already in his possession, Lincoln wrote and sealed a memorandum that he presented to the cabinet the same day. Without disclosing its contents, he requested that each member sign the back of the document. Only after the election did he reveal what it said:

This morning, as for some days past, it seems exceedingly probable that this Administration will not be re-elected. Then it will be my duty to so co-operate with the President elect, as to save the Union between the election and the inauguration; as he will have secured his election on such ground that he can not possibly save it afterwards.

In all likelihood, Lincoln chose not to share the contents of the Blind Memo because he realized, at least subconsciously, that it was an expression of emotion, not rational thought. By this late stage of the war, he was having more frequent nightmares and battling depressive moods. Yet by August 25, his mental state had shifted again. That day, he, Seward, Stanton, and Treasury Secretary William P. Fessenden (who had replaced Chase in July) met with Raymond at the White House. According to notes of presidential secretary John Nicolay, they "showed him [Raymond] that they had thoroughly considered and discussed the proposition of his letter of the 22d; and on giving him their reasons he very readily concurred with them in the opinion that to follow his plan of sending a commission to Richmond would be worse than losing the Presidential contest—it would be ignominiously surrendering it in advance. Nevertheless the visit of himself and committee here did great good. They found the President and Cabinet much better informed than themselves, and went home encouraged and cheered."

What Raymond and the members of his committee didn't know was that Sherman was about to capture Atlanta. In fact, when the Confederates began evacuating the city on September 1, their departure produced a much-celebrated Union victory that turned the political tide considerably. The behavior of the Democrats at their August 29–31 convention in Chicago also aided the president's cause.

The principal business of the convention was the nomination for president of George McClellan, whose antipathy toward Lincoln had only grown since his dismissal from command in November

President Lincoln's Blind Memo of August 23, 1864. The inset shows the signatures of the cabinet members on the back.

1862. Although known as a War Democrat, McClellan made himself acceptable to the Peace wing by promising to call for an immediate armistice upon his election.

Given the strength of the Peace Democrats within the party, McClellan had little choice. But accommodating their extremism also proved to be his undoing. As one Copperhead after another appeared on the convention dais to complain about the "flat-nosed, long-heeled cursed of God and damned of men descendants of Africa" who were despoiling the country, more and more voters realized that the Democratic party was not within the mainstream of Northern politics when it came to racial issues. Notably, the convention also brought into common usage a new term, *miscegenation*, which two Democratic journalists had recently coined to describe the interracial sexual congress being dangerously encouraged by Republican policies.

Even worse for McClellan, the Democratic platform adopted in Chicago contained a peace plank so odious to most Unionists that the general was forced immediately to repudiate it:

Resolved, That this convention does explicitly declare, as the sense of the American people, that after four years of failure to restore the Union by the experiment of war, during which, under the pretense of a military necessity of war-power higher than the Constitution, the Constitution itself has been disregarded in every part, and public liberty and private right alike trodden down, and the material prosperity of the country essentially impaired, justice, humanity, liberty, and the public welfare demand that immediate efforts be made for a cessation of hostilities, with a view of an ultimate convention of the States, or other peaceable means, to the end that, at the earliest practicable moment, peace may be restored on the basis of the Federal Union of the States.

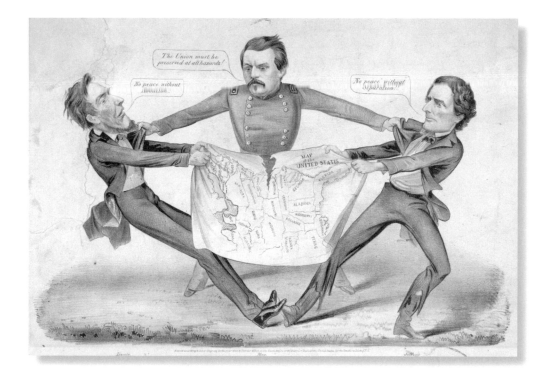

This 1864 pro-Democratic presidential campaign cartoon shows George B. McClellan acting as mediator in a tug-of-war between Abraham Lincoln and Jefferson Davis over a map of the United States. "The Union must be preserved at all hazards!" the former general says.

Meanwhile, Lincoln mended fences with the Radical Republicans. On September 23, he asked Montgomery Blair to resign from the cabinet. This completed a deal, brokered by Zachariah Chandler, in which Blair's dismissal was traded for Frémont's withdrawal from the presidential race.

When the votes were finally cast on November 8, the National Union coalition triumphed easily, receiving 55 percent of the popular tally and carrying all but three states (Delaware, Kentucky, and McClellan's home state of New Jersey). Lincoln thus became the first president to win a second term since Andrew Jackson in 1832. Remarkably, of the ballots cast by soldiers in army camps, the president won more than 70 percent. Apparently, they didn't believe the Democrats' contention that the war had been a failure.

We the People

of the United

insure domestic Tranquility, provide for the common defence, promote the ge

and our Posterity, do ordain and establish this Constitution for the United St

Article. 1.

Section. 1. All legislative Powers herein granted shall be vested in a Cong

of Representatives.

Section. 2. The House of Representatives shall be composed of Members chos

in each State shall have the Qualifications requisite for Electors of the most numerous Bra

No Person shall be a Representative who shall not have attained to the Age

and who shall not, when elected, be an Inhabitant of that State in which he shall be ch

Representatives and direct Taxes shall be apportioned among the several State

Numbers, which shall be determined by adding to the whole Number of free Persons, in

not taxed, three fifths of all other Persons. The actual Enumeration shall be made w

and within every subsequent Term of ten Years, in such Manner as they shall by Lav

thirty Thousand, but each State shall have at Least one Representative; and until s

entitled to chuse three, Massachusetts eight, Rhode-Island and Providence Plant

eight, Delaware one, Maryland six, Virginia ten, North Carolina five, South Car

When vacancies happen in the Representation from any State, the Executive

The House of Representatives shall chuse their Speaker and other Officers; an

Section. 3. The Senate of the United States shall be composed of two Senators fro

Senator shall have one Vote.

Immediately after they shall be assembled in Consequence of the first Electi

of the Senators of the first Class shall be vacated at the Expiration of the second Year,

Class at the Expiration of the sixth Year, so that one third may be chosen every second

Recess of the Legislature of any State, the Executive thereof may make temporary Appoin

such Vacancies.

No Person shall be a Senator who shall not have attained to the Age of thirty

not, when elected, be an Inhabitant of that State for which he shall be chosen.

The Vice President of the United States shall be President of the Senate, but shal

The Senate shall chuse their other Officers, and also a President pro tempore, in

President of the United States.

The Senate shall have the sole Power to try all Impeachments. When sitting

of the United States is tried, the Chief Justice shall preside: And no Person shall be convicted

IV

A Permanent Solution

❧

AS Abraham Lincoln well understood, the Emancipation Proclamation did not abolish the institution of slavery. In the border states and in the Union-controlled territory exempted from the proclamation, African Americans were still held in legal bondage. Even in the Confederacy, where all of the slaves had been nominally freed, no federal law prevented their reenslavement or the purchase of new slaves by Southern masters.

Lincoln was also aware of a second problem with the Emancipation Proclamation: its longevity was uncertain. At any time, a federal court could deem it unconstitutional; Congress could vote to overturn it; or a new president could choose to rescind it, as McClellan would likely have done had he been elected.

President Lincoln could have ignored these problems. With the Union now firmly on the path to victory, the "military necessity" argument for emancipation seemed much less compelling. It could have been rationalized, in fact, that the moment of necessity had passed. But Lincoln didn't think this way. Although he took his time before making a decision, once made he stuck to it. "I am charged with vacillating; but . . . I do not think that charge can be sustained," he once told Frederick Douglass. "I think it cannot be shown that when I have once taken a position, I have ever retreated from it."

Slavery had caused the war, Lincoln reasoned. Therefore, to end the war and prevent its recurrence, slavery needed to be ended as well. No peace could be lasting, the president believed, that permitted the continuance of human bondage. When the Confederacy was defeated,

OPPOSITE: **The original engrossed version of the Constitution approved in Philadelphia in 1787.**

perhaps within a few weeks of Lincoln's second inauguration, his war powers would cease. He needed to find a permanent solution before that happened.

The chief obstacle was the Constitution—which, the Supreme Court had ruled in *Dred Scott v. Sandford* (1857), prevented Congress from enacting any laws to limit slavery, much less abolish it. (In the view of the Court, slavery was subject to state law only.) The federal government could act only if the Constitution were changed, but that hadn't been done in sixty years.

If one considers the first ten constitutional amendments (the Bill of Rights) to be part of the original document—as their author, James Madison, intended—then the Constitution had been amended only twice before 1865, both times to correct obvious technical defects. The Eleventh Amendment, ratified in 1795, remedied an oversight on the part of the framers, who had neglected to provide the states with the same sovereign immunity granted the federal government. The Twelfth Amendment, ratified in 1804, likewise fixed a procedural problem that had allowed Aaron Burr to contest Jefferson's election as president in 1800. Since then, a few other amendments had been proposed—including one by John Quincy Adams in 1839 to abolish slavery—but only two of these had passed Congress, and neither had been ratified.

The reason for this constitutional stasis was that most people had become "Constitution worshipers," to use the contemporary phrase. During the first half of the nineteenth century, Americans came to hold the framers in such high, almost religious, regard that the great majority were loath to change a single word they had written. Observed abolitionist Lydia Maria Child in 1862, "Wholesale lauding of the Constitution has made it an object of idol-worship." Lincoln had this hurdle to overcome as well.

**Ohio representative
James M. Ashley**

**Illinois senator
Lyman Trumbull**

**Massachusetts senator
Charles Sumner**

A S it happened, the Thirty-eighth Congress had already taken up an antislavery amendment. On December 14, 1863, Ohio Radical James M. Ashley had introduced a joint resolution in the House calling for a constitutional amendment to abolish slavery. Because Lincoln was then pursuing a different legal strategy—emancipation through changes to state law, not federal law—the administration didn't show much interest in Ashley's resolution. Neither did most of Ashley's colleagues in the House. But the introduction of a similar resolution in the Senate on January 11, 1864—because it came from an unexpected source—stirred that body into action.

The sponsor of the Senate resolution, John B. Henderson of Missouri, was a former slaveholder with no love for African Americans and no care for their rights. Rather, he was a War Democrat who had supported the National Union ticket because he had believed it was in his political interest to do so. Similarly, he now supported an antislavery amendment because he wanted to put an end to "the Negro issue" dividing both his state and the nation. Following Senate procedure, Henderson's resolution was referred to the Judiciary Committee, chaired by Illinois Republican Lyman Trumbull.

While Trumbull and his committee colleagues began to consider what form the amendment should take, Charles Sumner (not a Judiciary Committee member) schemed to gain control of the amendment for himself.

On February 8, the Radical senator from Massachusetts introduced a second antislavery resolution, asking that it be referred to the Committee on Slavery and Freedom, which he chaired. Because doing so would have violated the well-established practice of sending constitutional amendments to the Judiciary Committee, and also because Sumner was not well liked by his colleagues, the request was denied. However, Sumner's stratagem did prompt the Judiciary Committee to move ahead more quickly; and two days later, Trumbull announced that the committee had completed its work.

In his February 8 resolution, Sumner had proposed this language for the amendment:

*All persons are equal before the law, so that
no person can hold another as a slave: and the
Congress shall have the power to make all laws
necessary and proper to carry this declaration into
effect everywhere within the United States and the
jurisdiction thereof.*

For reasons that were obvious to observers in 1864 (if less so to readers today), Sumner's formulation antagonized both War Democrats and conservative Republicans. Consider, for example, Sumner's choice of terminology. Because U.S. senators of the nineteenth century were generally well-educated men of privilege, they would have

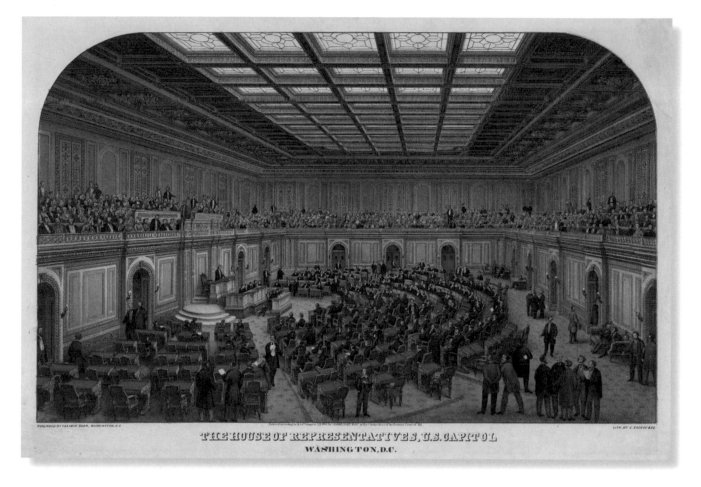

An interior view of the House in 1866, showing the members in session and spectators in the gallery.

recognized the origin of the concept "equality before the law" in the 1789 Declaration of the Rights of Man and of the Citizen, the founding document of the French Revolution—which American conservatives of the 1860s considered overreaching radicalism. "I would not go to the French Revolution to find the proper words for a constitution," Trumbull scolded Sumner on the floor of the Senate. "We all know that their constitutions were failures, while ours, we trust, will be permanent." Much more significantly, making the amendment applicable to "all persons" would have wrought a legal revolution at a time when most Americans (that is, women) did not yet enjoy equality before the law.

Instead, for guidance, the Judiciary Committee looked to the Northwest Ordinance of 1787, penned by Jefferson to create the Northwest Territory beyond the Ohio River. Article VI of that ordinance prohibited slavery in the new territory: "There shall be neither slavery nor involuntary servitude in the said territory, otherwise than in the

punishment of crimes whereof the party shall have been duly convicted." This language had two principal virtues: it was simple; and, having served as the basis of many state antislavery laws, it had been thoroughly adjudicated.

The text reported out by the Judiciary Committee read as follows:

> *Section 1. Neither slavery nor involuntary servitude, except as a punishment for crime whereof the party shall have been duly convicted, shall exist within the United States, or any place subject to their jurisdiction.*

> *Section 2. Congress shall have power to enforce this article by appropriate legislation.*

In a vote taken April 8, 1864, the Senate approved the amendment, 38–6, easily reaching the necessary two-thirds majority. The nays belonged to the four senators from

This portrait of Lincoln was taken at Mathew Brady's Washington studio on January 8, 1864, during one of three visits the president made to the studio that year.

for a final vote on June 15, he switched his vote to nay, thereby gaining the right to move the amendment's reconsideration at some future point in the deliberations of the Thirty-eighth Congress. Only three weeks remained in the current session, but a second session was scheduled to begin in December 1864, after the presidential election, and Ashley remained hopeful that the political situation might change. It did.

WITH more than cursory justification, Lincoln interpreted his impressive 1864 victory as a definitive popular endorsement not only of his emancipation policy but also of the Republican/National Union platform, in which the Radicals had inserted a strongly worded plank calling for passage of the antislavery amendment. The president was also feeling particularly influential, given that a horde of new Republican congressmen had been elected on his coattails. In his annual message to Congress of December 6, 1864, he flexed this new political muscle, affirming his personal support for the amendment and making a political argument for its immediate passage that was a bit coy but undeniably clear:

Delaware and Kentucky plus Democrats from California and Indiana. The ayes included all thirty-one Republicans, two Oregon Democrats, and five border-state Unionists.

In the House, however, the Democrats' gains in the 1862 elections gave them more than enough strength to block the amendment. By Ashley's count, he had only 93 of the 122 votes needed for passage (barring abstentions). Facing certain defeat, he employed a parliamentary trick. When the amendment came to the floor of the House

At the last session of Congress a proposed amendment of the Constitution abolishing slavery throughout the United States passed the Senate, but failed for lack of the requisite two-thirds vote in the House of Representatives. Although the present is the same Congress and nearly the same members, and without questioning the wisdom or patriotism of those who stood in opposition, I venture to recommend the reconsideration and passage of the measure at the present session. Of course the abstract question is not changed; but an intervening election shows almost certainly that the next Congress will pass the measure if this does not. Hence there is only a question of time as to when the proposed amendment will go to the States for their action. And as it is to so go at all events, may we not agree that the sooner the better?

RESOLVED, That as slavery was the cause, and now constitutes the strength of this Rebellion, and as it must be, always and everywhere, hostile to the principles of Republican Government, justice and the National safety demand its utter and complete extirpation from the soil of the Republic; and that, while we uphold and maintain the acts and proclamations by which the Government, in its own defense, has aimed a deathblow at this gigantic evil, we are in favor, furthermore, of such an amendment to the Constitution, to be made by the people in conformity with its provisions, as shall terminate and forever prohibit the existence of Slavery within the limits of the jurisdiction of the United States.

(Republican/National Union party platform, June 7, 1864)

Once Ashley moved for reconsideration of the amendment in the

House, the fight was on. The Ohio representative managed the legislation within the chamber, while Secretary of State Seward supervised the administration's lobbying effort.

The ideological cleavages that confronted Ashley and Seward were difficult to navigate, even for political professionals. But the mathematics of the situation were clear. There were 86 Republican votes in the House. Even if all 24 Unionists voted aye as well (which wasn't likely), the amendment would still fall 12 votes short of passage. At least a dozen Democrats would have to vote for it.

In some ways, factionalism helped the amendment. The division between the War and Peace Democrats, exacerbated by McClellan's disastrous candidacy, made the former much easier targets for conversion, especially the lame ducks among them. On the other hand, factionalism among the Republicans threatened to derail the effort. Animosity between the Radical and conservative (Blair) factions of the party, suppressed while the fate of the Union hung in the balance, now emerged with victory at hand. Just three months earlier, the Radicals had forced Montgomery Blair's dismissal from the cabinet; and the postmaster general (understanding full well Lincoln's position) blamed the Radicals, not the president. Fortunately, both camps favored passage of the amendment, each for its own reasons.

The Radicals' reasoning was simple: they wanted the amendment to serve as a foundation for far-reaching Reconstruction legislation that would guarantee the freedpeople equality before the law. The Blairs had a more byzantine strategy. Their ultimate purpose was the same—to influence Reconstruction—but they wanted to limit African-American rights in the postwar world. Actively lobbying on the amendment's behalf, Montgomery Blair argued that conservative Republicans and War Democrats should support immediate emancipation because its defeat

Montgomery Blair believed the Radicals were overestimating the ability of former slaves to thrive as free people.

would give the Radicals a pretext for much more intrusive interference in state affairs. Rather than fight abolition, he advised, with public opinion against them, they should fall back to the much firmer ground of postabolition race relations.

During the House's Christmas recess, Ashley surveyed the membership and counted 108 votes in favor of the amendment, 14 shy of passage. Next, he made a list of 19 congressmen he believed might be susceptible to persuasion. Even if he couldn't change their nay votes to ayes, he might be able to switch them to abstentions, thus lowering the number of votes necessary to obtain the two-thirds majority *of members in attendance.* For every three abstentions he and Seward arranged, the number of ayes required would drop by two.

James M. Ashley sent this printed circular to members of the House during the 1864 Christmas recess to build support for the Thirteenth Amendment. He often added handwritten notes to congressmen he knew personally.

WASHINGTON, D. C.,

December 25th, 1864.

DEAR SIR :

The importance of the vote to be taken in the House Monday, January 9th, on the Constitutional Amendment, cannot be overestimated. If every member known to be in favor of the Amendment is present on that day, the vote for it will be one hundred and eight, including the Speaker.

Of the Opposition, *nineteen* are set down as doubtful. Eight or ten of this number we hope will vote for the proposition, and the others may voluntarily absent themselves.

Fifty-six members are regarded as sure to vote against us, if they are present. It is believed, however, that quite a number of gentlemen classed as certainly against us, desire the Amendment to pass, if it can be done, without their votes. If they are present, however, they will vote against it.

I need not press upon you the necessity of your presence in the city on Saturday, the 7th inst.

If from any cause you are uncertain as to whether you can be present or not, please telegraph some member of the Opposition at once, and secure a pair, and as soon as you secure one, telegraph the fact to me, and have whoever you pair with telegraph me also, so that I may know Saturday night exactly how the vote will stand.

Pardon me if I make another suggestion. If you can, through some personal friend, have the Opposition papers in your locality throughout the State, come out daily for a number of days in favor of letting the Amendment pass, claiming that its passage would forever dispose of the slavery agitation, I think it would secure us some votes which we cannot now hope for.

Respectfully,

J. M. ASHLEY.

This view of Broadway in New York City looking south from City Hall Park was published by Currier & Ives.

To bring more resources to bear, Seward organized a team of well-connected private lobbyists to pursue Democratic votes. The four principal members were a Tennessean and three New Yorkers. Nashville lawyer and land speculator William N. Bilbo had made Seward's acquaintance decades earlier when both men were up-and-coming Whigs. Although Bilbo had initially supported the Confederacy, he switched his allegiance during 1864 for some unknown reason and left the South for New York City. George O. Jones was a high-priced professional lobbyist, active in both Albany and Washington, whose ethically challenged clients included railroad magnate Cornelius Vanderbilt and stock speculator Daniel Drew. Robert W. Latham was born in Virginia but moved as a young man to New York City, where he became a banker and stockbroker and a close friend of Seward. During the Buchanan administration, Latham frequently acted as a conduit between financial speculators and influential Democratic politicians, not always with the public

interest in mind. Richard Schell, another denizen of Wall Street, had strong connections to Tammany Hall, the city's Democratic political machine.

The motives of these men are obscure. They may have been seeking political favors for themselves. They may have been acting out of a sincere desire to serve the Union or help their friend Seward. All of the above may have been true. In any case, they began lobbying in early December. Bilbo operated primarily in Washington and Jones in Albany, while Latham and Schell worked in both New York City and the national capital. In mid-December, for example, Jones met with New York governor Horatio Seymour, the most prominent Democrat in the country after McClellan, and Dean Richmond, the kingmaker who ran the Albany Regency, one of the oldest and most powerful Democratic organizations in the country. According to Jones' report, conveyed to Seward by Bilbo, Seymour and Richmond were ambivalent about the amendment. On the one hand, they were concerned that its passage might disrupt the balance of power between the states and the federal government. On the other, they knew that "no party [in the] North can maintain its political status that opposes it." In the end, Jones obtained their commitment to remain neutral, advising neither support nor rejection to New York's seventeen Democratic congressmen.

The lobbyists remained busy throughout the rest of December, but in early January their efforts stalled. "The discussions in Congress are not aiding us," Bilbo reported to Seward. "The most strenuous efforts are made by the Leaders of the Democracy, to unite every member in the House against the Amendment." On January 10, while meeting informally with several reporters, Speaker of the House Schuyler Colfax, an Indiana Republican, remarked that he thought the measure was still five votes short of passage. Ashley must have agreed because he had already pushed back the floor vote from January 9 to January 31.

Aware of the difficulties his lobbyists were encountering, the president became much more personally involved. In fact, never before had Lincoln intervened so directly in the affairs of Congress. His preferred method was to invite wavering members over to the White House for private chats. At one such meeting with a House member whose brother had been killed in the war, Lincoln said, "Your brother died to save the Republic from death by the slave-holders' rebellion. I wish you could see it to be your duty to vote for the constitutional amendment ending slavery."

Not always, however, was the president so polite. According to Massachusetts Republican John B. Alley, Lincoln summoned two other representatives to the White House and ordered them to find two more votes for the amendment. When they asked him how he expected them to do this, Lincoln replied, "I leave it to you to determine how it shall be done; but remember that I am President of the United States, clothed with immense power, and I expect you to procure those votes."

Meanwhile, Ashley and Seward continued to troll for votes, both understanding that the president didn't want to know what promises they were making in his name—at least not until after the amendment had passed. Nevertheless, Ashley did approach Lincoln in mid-January with an unusual request. The congressman had been contacted by agents of the Camden & Amboy Railroad, which held a state monopoly on the only rail line running the entire length of New Jersey. Antimonopolists in the Senate, led by Charles Sumner, had introduced a bill establishing a competitive railroad in New Jersey, thus stripping the Camden & Amboy of its unfair advantage. If Sumner could be persuaded to postpone this bill until the next Congress, Ashley was told, the Camden & Amboy would gratefully return the favor by using its influence with several New Jersey Democrats to change their votes.

Because Ashley had no influence with Sumner, he took the offer to Nicolay, who briefed the president.

Nicolay reported that the president rejected the offer, saying, "I can do nothing with Mr. Sumner in these matters." But the intrigue didn't end there, according to the story later passed around Capitol Hill. Andrew J. Rogers was a New Jersey Democrat whose opposition to the amendment was as strong and widely known as were his ties to the Camden & Amboy. When Rogers failed to appear in the House on the day of the vote, Missouri Unionist James S. Rollins,

The corner of 15th and F streets in Washington, less than two blocks from the White House, as it appeared in April 1865.

Mathew Brady took this photograph of the south side of the White House (then ungated) during the Civil War.

who had been working closely with Lincoln on the lobbying effort, announced that Rogers had been "confined to his room several days by indisposition." That the information came from Rollins suggested collusion of the highest order—a suspicion confirmed to most insiders when the Senate Commerce Committee failed to report out Sumner's bill before the end of the session.

"The wish or order of the President is very potent. He can punish and reward," a member of the opposition observed during the House debate. Yet Lincoln's participation in the Camden & Amboy affair is purely speculative. "There is not one reliable source, nor even an unreliable one, that reports the president making any specific promise in exchange for a vote for the amendment," Michael Vorenberg concluded in his comprehensive study of the Thirteenth Amendment and its passage. Rather, Vorenberg explained, "Lincoln let his lieutenants make the bargains and use his name to seal the agreement. This arrangement kept the president uninvolved in shady negotiations while giving tremendous bargaining power to Ashley, Seward, and others working for the amendment."

Some of the negotiations certainly skirted the law. Latham had been implicated in bribery scandals before, and he may again have offered cash to congressmen. In a January 9 letter to Seward he wrote, "Money will certainly do it, if patriotism fails." The secretary of state doesn't seem to have objected.

WHILE the Seward lobby and others worked behind the scenes, the members of the House debated the amendment publicly on the floor. Their speeches brought up several issues that would later become the focus of much Reconstruction legislation, especially the question of whether the freedmen should enjoy equality before the law.

No one doubted that the Radicals wanted to take the issue as far as they could, because they believed that African Americans deserved to compete economically on a level playing field with whites. But the Radicals were shrewd enough to realize that pushing too hard, too fast, would cause a backlash and chase moderates into the Blair camp. So, when necessary, they evaded and temporized.

For example, when Democrats insisted that the antislavery amendment was but a prelude to black suffrage, Republicans adamantly denied the charge. "A recognition of natural rights is one thing; a grant of political franchise is quite another," John R. McBride of Oregon declared. "If political rights must necessarily follow the possession of personal liberty, then all but male citizens in our country are slaves." Similarly, when Ohio Democrat Samuel "Sunset" Cox challenged Thaddeus Stevens of Pennsylvania to explain where he stood on Negro equality—even though everyone knew where he stood—the Radical champion hedged:

Pennsylvania representative
Thaddeus Stevens

I AM not, sir, one of those who believe that the emancipation of the black race is of itself to elevate them to an equality with the white race. I believe in the distinction of race as existing in the providence of God for his wise and beneficent designs to man; but I would make every race free and equal before the law, permitting to each the elevation to which its own capacity and culture should entitle it, and securing to each the fruits of its own progression. This we can do only by removing every vestige of African slavery from the American Republic.

—THOMAS T. DAVIS
(New York Republican's speech on the floor of the House, January 7, 1865)

Mr. COX. Will he not give up something on his part? Give up his doctrine of negro equality? Give up his idea of breaking down State institutions by Federal law?

Mr. STEVENS. The gentleman will allow me to say that I never held to that doctrine of negro equality.

Mr. COX. Then I understand the gentleman from Pennsylvania not to hold that all men are created equal?

Mr. STEVENS. Yes, sir, but not equality in all things—simply before the law, nothing else.

Beyond the halls of Congress, the public debated the issue as well. Now that the war finally seemed to be ending, Americans were eager to make some sense of what had happened and to understand where the country now stood. In this politically fertile climate, it no longer seemed quite so sacrilegious to consider changing the text of the Constitution, despite the framers' obvious intent to allow slavery. In fact, changing the Constitution began to seem quite appealing.

"Northerners blamed the South for the carnage [of the war], but they also now channeled their anger toward the founders, who had allowed the cause of the war, slavery, to survive," Vorenberg wrote. "Indeed, as the prospect of sectional reunion became more real, northerners found it easier to point their fingers at long-dead framers

Jefferson Davis and his wife, Varina, moved at the top levels of Washington society when Davis was a senator and later secretary of war in the Pierce administration.

than at the southerners who would be their brethren in a reconstructed Union. The amendment was thus a swipe at the founders and a sign that, as [journalist E. L.] Godkin put it, 'the spell [of the Constitution] has been broken by the war.'"

OF the Democrats' many arguments against the amendment, the most influential was the claim that its passage would scuttle the possibility of peace negotiations with the South. This carried little weight with the Radicals, who were not interested in a negotiated settlement. But more moderate Northerners weren't so sure. The loss of life during the 1864 campaign had been so egregious that most people winced at the thought of what might occur in 1865. If the death of one more father, son, or brother could be avoided, shouldn't the government at least explore peace negotiations with the Confederacy?

For Lincoln, the issue was a trap. There was no real basis for negotiation, he knew, because restoration of the Union and abandonment of slavery, the war aims on which he wouldn't budge, were both unacceptable terms to the Confederacy. On the other hand, if Lincoln rejected negotiations out of hand, he risked seeming unreasonable, to the detriment of his party and the benefit of the Copperheads. Being a clever politician, the president adopted a third course, occasionally authorizing private

citizens (including Horace Greeley in July 1864) to meet with Confederate representatives, always confident that the meetings would come to naught.

Lincoln employed this strategy again on December 28, 1864, when Francis Preston Blair, Sr., met with him at the White House to request a pass through the Union lines. Blair wanted to go to Richmond, he said, to retrieve personal papers that had been taken from his Silver Spring estate during Jubal Early's July raid. There was a covert purpose to the visit as well: Confederate president Jefferson Davis was an old friend, and Blair intended to present Davis with a secret plan for peace. He started to explain this to Lincoln, but the president stopped him, not wanting to know.

Lincoln had two good reasons to grant Blair's request. The first was the same reason he had decided to permit Greeley's July escapade: he hoped that Southern rejection of his two preconditions for negotiation (reunion and emancipation) would shatter the Northern illusion that peace could be negotiated with the South and prove, once and for all, that the only way for the Union to achieve its war aims was through military victory. (Should continued Confederate intransigence cause Southerners to begin doubting the good judgment of their own leaders, so much the better.) The second reason was that Lincoln needed the goodwill of the Blairs to solidify conservative Republican support for the antislavery amendment.

Arriving in Richmond on January 12, the seventy-three-year-old Blair met with Davis that evening to lay out his peace proposal. Its essence was that the North and South would declare an immediate armistice and combine

Allow the bearer, F. P. Blair, Senr. to pass our lines, go South and return

A. Lincoln

Dec. 28. 1864

This is the "passport" that Lincoln gave Francis Preston Blair, Sr., to facilitate his passage through the Union lines.

The classical Virginia State Capitol (then the Confederate capitol) rises above Richmond in this wartime view.

their armies for the purpose of repulsing French adventurism in Mexico. Blair believed that joining forces against a common enemy would rekindle the bonds of national affection and serve as a natural prelude to reunion. As for slavery, Blair said, it "no longer remains an insurmountable obstruction" because "the cause of all our woes is admitted now on all sides to be doomed."

Davis politely agreed that "no circumstances would have a greater effect [on reconciliation] than to see the arms of our countrymen from the North and the South united in a war upon a foreign power assailing principles of government common to both sections." Nevertheless, he told Blair, he could not support a joint military expedition at this time; the Mexicans would have to drive out the French themselves.

This statement seemed to end the discussion, yet Davis kept talking. Apparently, he was concerned himself that charges of intransigence would undermine his standing, so he told Blair that, Mexico aside, he was willing to appoint a delegation to meet with Lincoln to discuss an end to the war. Ultimately, he gave Blair a letter stating that "I have no disposition to find obstacles in forms, and am willing now, as heretofore, to enter into negotiations for the restoration of peace . . . I would, if you could promise that a commissioner, minister or other agent would be received, appoint one immediately, and renew the effort to enter into a conference with a view to secure peace to the two countries."

Blair returned to Washington with this letter on January 16, meeting with the president two days later.

Although excited and hopeful, he realized that Davis' final phrase would be a problem. There was no way that Lincoln could accept the "two countries" formulation because it gainsaid Lincoln's own carefully maintained position that the Confederacy was not an independent country. Nevertheless, the president was intrigued, both by Davis' letter and Blair's report of widespread despondency in the Confederate capital. In the end, Lincoln chose to pursue the opening a little farther, hoping that he might be able to increase the internal pressure on Davis. He asked Blair to return to Richmond with a carefully crafted reply. It was addressed to Blair, rather than Davis, because Lincoln would not recognize formally the authority of the Confederate president.

"You may say to him," Lincoln wrote on January 18, "that I have constantly been, am now, and shall continue, ready to receive any agent whom he, or any other influential person now resisting the national authority, may informally send to me with a view to securing peace to the people of our one common country."

By this time, of course, news of Blair's visit to Richmond had spread throughout the capital and the country, leading to all sorts of wild speculation. "That the Blair Mission has become the national excitement is evident enough from [reading] the leading press of the country," the *Washington National Intelligencer* observed; while the *New York Herald* reported on January 21, just ten days before the amendment vote, that the capital "has been under an intense excitement during the last few days over the question of peace. All manner of probable and improbable, possible and impossible stories have been in circulation."

Blair returned to Richmond on January 20, presenting Lincoln's letter to Davis the following day. After allowing Davis time to read the letter twice, Blair told the Confederate president that Lincoln would not compromise on the one-country formulation as a condition for peace talks. Davis gave Blair no reply. However, on January 27, the day after Blair left Richmond, Davis called Confederate vice president Alexander H. Stephens (formerly a U.S. congressman from Georgia) into his office to discuss a matter of "special and important business." Davis shared Lincoln's letter with Stephens, who agreed that perhaps it meant an armistice could be arranged.

On January 28, after obtaining the approval of his cabinet, Davis appointed three peace commissioners to "proceed to Washington City for an informal conference with [Mr. Lincoln] upon the issues involved in the existing war, and for the purpose of securing peace to the two countries." The delegation included Stephens, former U.S. senator Robert M. T. Hunter (now a Confederate senator), and former Supreme Court justice John A. Campbell (now Davis' assistant secretary of war).

On January 29, the Confederate peace commissioners presented themselves at Petersburg, seeking permission to enter the Union lines. The surprised officer in command on the front, Maj. Gen. O. B. Wilcox, didn't know what to do, so he telegraphed Grant's headquarters at City Point, Virginia, for instructions. In Grant's temporary absence,

Alexander H. Stephens   Robert M. T. Hunter   John A. Campbell

This view of Fortress Monroe in 1862 shows the bustle of wartime activity in the waters of Hampton Roads.

Wilcox's message was rerouted to Maj. Gen. Edward O. C. Ord, who had replaced Butler as commander of the Army of the James. Ord didn't know what to do, either, so he sent the request on to Secretary of War Stanton, who referred it to the president. This took some time, during which Grant returned to his headquarters and granted the commissioners entry to the Union lines, after which he had them conveycd to City Point.

When Lincoln learned of this development the following day, he ordered Grant to detain Stephens, Hunter, and Campbell at City Point "in comfortable quarters" until they could be interviewed by Maj. Thomas T. Eckert, whom the president was dispatching from Washington. Lincoln's orders to Eckert instructed the major to show the Confederate commissioners his letter to Blair of January 18 containing the "one country" condition, ask them whether they accepted it, and "receive their answer in writing."

On the morning of January 31, shortly before Eckert's departure, Lincoln decided to send Secretary of State Seward to Fortress Monroe. The president had no intention of allowing the peace commissioners into Washington; but, if their response to Eckert was positive, he would allow them to meet with Seward at a midpoint, and Hampton Roads seemed the most convenient spot. Ironically, the president was composing his instructions to Seward when he received an urgent note from James Ashley.

ASHLEY had gone to bed on January 30 fairly certain that he had enough votes for passage. However, when he returned to Capitol Hill on the morning of the vote, he was no longer so sure. A seemingly credible rumor that three Confederate peace commissioners were on their way to Washington (or perhaps were already there!) had unsettled the House. If the rumor proved to be true, many hard-won Democratic votes would surely revert to nays. An anxious Ashley quickly messengered this note to Lincoln at the White House:

> The report is in circulation in the House that Peace Commissioners are on their way or in the city, and is being used against us. If it is true, I fear we shall lose the bill. Please authorize me to contradict it, if it is not true.

Lincoln interrupted his work on Seward's instruction to read Ashley's note. He replied immediately on the same piece of paper:

So far as I know there are no peace Commissioners in the city or likely to be in it. A. LINCOLN.

When Lincoln's reply reached Capitol Hill, Ashley read it aloud on the floor of the House, and the message had its desired effect, calming the members. Were it not for Lincoln's assurance, Ashley later observed to former Lincoln law partner William H. Herndon, who was writing a posthumous biography of the president, "I think the proposed amendment would have failed, as a number who voted for it could easily have been prevailed upon to vote against it, on the ground that the passage of such a proposition would be offensive to the Commissioners.

"Mr. Lincoln knew that the Commissioners were then on their way to Fortress Monroe, where he expected to meet them, and afterwards did meet them," Ashley continued. "You see how he answered my note for my purposes, and yet how truly. You know how he afterwards met the so-called commission, whom he determined at the time he wrote this note should not come to the city."

Rather than allow the months-long lobbying effort to collapse, Lincoln chose to move ahead in a way that ensured even greater momentum for the amendment. To wit, shortly after the reading of the president's message, according to journalist Noah Brooks, "Archibald McAllister, a Pennsylvania Peace Democrat, astonished everybody by sending up to the clerk's desk a note in which he said that as all peace negotiations and missions had failed, he was satisfied that nothing short of their independence would satisfy the Southern Confederates, and he therefore determined to cast his vote against the cornerstone of the Southern Confederacy—slavery." Several other Democrats and border-state Unionists who had previously withheld their support soon followed McAllister's example. Finally, shortly after three o'clock, Speaker of the House Colfax intoned, "Shall the joint resolution pass?"

Gallery regulars couldn't recall when the House had been so crowded. As the call of the roll commenced, members gathered together in knots around colleagues who were keeping tallies. The Copperheads gathered about their leader, George H. Pendleton of Ohio, whom Brooks described as "looking gloomy, black and sour." Meanwhile, in the packed galleries, the large antislavery contingent cheered loudly each time a Democrat or border-state Unionist voted aye. The wildest applause came after John Ganson of New York, well known as a Peace Democrat, cast an especially surprising aye. The amendment's passage, it seemed, was now assured.

When Colfax announced the final result— 119 ayes, 56 nays, and 8 abstentions—there was initially an incredulous silence. Then came a spasm of emotion that no one who experienced it ever forgot. The reaction in the House "begged description," Indiana Republican George W. Julian wrote in his diary. "Members joined in the shouting and kept it up for some minutes. Some embraced one another, others wept like children. I have felt, ever since the vote, as if I were in a new country."

Although most of the spectators were white, there were also some blacks in the audience, and they were doubly moved—once by the passage of the amendment and a second time by the reaction of the euphoric whites.

Presidential private secretary John G. Nicolay passed this message to Lincoln reporting the vote count on the passage of the Thirteenth Amendment.

HARPER'S WEEKLY.
JOURNAL OF CIVILIZATION

Vol. IX.—No. 425.] NEW YORK, SATURDAY, FEBRUARY 18, 1865. [SINGLE COPIES TEN CENTS. $4.00 PER YEAR IN ADVANCE.

SCENE IN THE HOUSE ON THE PASSAGE OF THE PROPOSITION TO AMEND THE CONSTITUTION, JANUARY 31, 1865.

The front page of the February 18, 1865, issue of *Harper's Weekly* depicted the riotously jubilant scene in the House of Representatives following passage of the Thirteenth Amendment.

FOR a moment there was a pause of utter silence, as if the voices of the dense mass of spectators were choked by strong emotion. Then there was an explosion, a storm of cheers, the like of which probably no Congress of the United States ever heard before. Strong men embraced each other with tears. The galleries and aisles were bristling with standing, cheering crowds. The air was stirred with a cloud of women's handkerchiefs waving and floating; hands were shaking; men threw their arms about each other's necks; and cheer after cheer, and burst after burst followed. Full ten minutes elapsed before silence returned sufficient to enable Ebon C. Ingersoll, of Illinois, to move an adjournment "in honor of the sublime and immortal event," upon which B. C. Harris, the deeply censured Marylander, shaking with wrath, arose and demanded the ayes and noes on the motion. This little artifice to procure delay did not amount to much, for, as the roll call began, members answered to their names and passed out, most of the defeated Copperheads taking their hats and stealing away before their names were reached. As the roll call went on amidst great confusion (for there was no longer any pretense of maintaining order), the air was rent by the thunder of a great salute fired on Capitol Hill, to notify all who heard that slavery was no more.

—NOAH BROOKS
Washington in Lincoln's Time (1895)

Frederick Douglass' son Charles, a Union army veteran, was present in the gallery, and he wrote to his father describing what he saw: "I wish you could have been here the day that the constitutional amendment was passed forever abolishing slavery in the United States, such rejoicing I never before witnessed, cannon firing, people hugging and shaking hands, white people I mean. . . . I tell you things are progressing finely."

Another black spectator chose to express his elation more privately. He found an empty anteroom not far from the House chamber and danced a solitary jig of jubilation.

V

Blood Enough Shed

~

THE Confederate peace commissioners lingered for two days at City Point. Grant described their stay in his memoirs, written shortly before his death in 1885. "Our relations were pleasant and I found them all very agreeable gentlemen," he wrote. "I directed the captain [of the dispatch boat *Mary Martin*] to furnish them with the best the boat afforded, and to administer to their comfort in every way possible. No guard was placed over them and no restriction was put upon their movements; nor was there any pledge asked that they would not abuse the privileges extended to them. They were permitted to leave the boat when they felt like it, and did so, coming up on the bank and visiting me at my headquarters."

According to Grant, no matters of substance were discussed. "I saw them quite frequently, though I have no recollection of having had any conversation whatever with them on the subject of their mission," he wrote. "It was something I had nothing to do with, and I therefore did not wish to express any views on the subject."

This account was certainly untrue.

When Major Eckert arrived at City Point on February 1, he met immediately with the Confederate commissioners. The meeting took place at 4:15 P.M. Following Lincoln's instructions, Eckert showed them the president's letter of January 18 and asked them to acknowledge in writing its precondition of reunion. Their reply came at 6 P.M. Because it contained evasive language, the punctilious major judged it "not satisfactory."

At 8 P.M., while Eckert prepared his report for the president, the commissioners contacted Grant. "We desire

to go to Washington City to confer informally with the President personally," their message read, "in reference to the matters mentioned in his letter to Mr. Blair of the 18th of January ultimo, without any personal compromise on any question in the letter." But Grant had no authority in the matter, and Eckert wouldn't budge. At 9:30 P.M., Eckert informed the Confederates that they could proceed no farther; and half an hour later, he sent his report to Washington.

Reading the major's report early the next morning, Lincoln prepared to recall both Eckert and Seward. However, before he could issue the orders, he was interrupted by Secretary of War Stanton, who had received an urgent message from Grant—sent at 10:30 P.M. the previous evening, half an hour after Eckert sent his report.

Notwithstanding his later denial, Grant had indeed been taking part in substantive talks with the Confederates—enough so to persuade him that the commissioners' desire for peace was sufficient to accommodate reunion. Rather than allow Eckert's strictness to close the door to a settlement that might avert more bloodshed, Grant felt compelled to send the following telegram to Stanton:

Now that the interview between Major Eckert, under his written instructions, and Mr. Stephens and party has ended, I will state confidentially, but not officially to become a matter of record, that I am convinced, upon conversation with Messrs. Stephens and Hunter, that their intentions are good and their desire sincere to restore peace and union. I have not felt myself at liberty to express even views of my own or to account for my reticency. This has placed me in an awkward position, which I could have avoided by

Secretary of War
Edwin M. Stanton

Lt. Gen. Ulysses S. Grant

Maj. Thomas T. Eckert

not seeing them in the first instance. I fear now their going back without any expression from any one in authority will have a bad influence. At the same time I recognize the difficulties in the way of receiving these informal commissioners at this time, and do not know what to recommend. I am sorry, however, that Mr. Lincoln cannot have an interview with the two named in this dispatch, if not all three now within our lines. Their letter to me was all that the President's instructions contemplated, to secure their safe conduct, if they had used the same language to Major Eckert.

A copy of the telegram Lincoln sent to Grant instructing the general to tell the Confederate peace commissioners that he will meet them at Fortress Monroe.

"The dispatch of General Grant changed my purpose," Lincoln later told Congress. Immediately, he sent two new telegrams. One went to Fortress Monroe, informing Seward that the president would be joining him at Hampton Roads "as soon as I can come." The other went to Grant at City Point: "Say to the gentlemen I will meet them personally at Fortress Monroe as soon as I can get there." Lincoln departed Washington just two hours later, accompanied only by a valet and a single overnight bag.

Why the sudden change of mind? Lincoln never revealed his thinking, so all one can do is speculate. The shift may actually have been more emotional than rational. As Lincoln surely understood, the most likely outcome of Eckert's mission had always been failure. The president knew how personally obdurate Jefferson Davis could be and how committed Davis was to the goal of Southern independence. Therefore, Lincoln must also have realized that, whatever diplomatic niceties the commissioners were employing at City Point, the Confederacy remained resistant to reunion, as Eckert had clearly determined.

Yet, reading the major's reports, Lincoln was almost certainly disappointed. Like Grant, he regretted deeply the carnage of the war; and he must have wished, even if irrationally, for a deus ex machina that could stop it. Thus, it may well have been that Lincoln granted the commissioners a pass to Fortress Monroe primarily because he needed to pacify his own conscience. As a practical matter, he couldn't have expected the conference to yield much; but because it *might* yield something, he couldn't allow the opportunity to pass.

The journey from Washington to Hampton Roads was itself an adventure. The season being the depth of winter, the Potomac was clogged with ice, making navigation too treacherous for the president. Instead, he rode a special train to Annapolis, where he boarded the steamer *Thomas Colyer*. (In a hurry, Lincoln walked the entire half mile from the train station to the naval academy dock rather than wait for a carriage.) According to a *New York Herald* correspondent who happened to be aboard the *Thomas Colyer*, "We encountered large fields of ice, through which we passed slowly." A little after ten o'clock that night, the ship arrived off Fortress Monroe. Immediately, Lincoln transferred to the *River Queen*, where he learned from Seward and Eckert that the peace commissioners were anchored nearby aboard the *Mary Martin*.

Word of the president's hasty departure from Washington startled the capital. When Republicans realized what was happening, their reaction was mostly negative. "None of the Cabinet were advised of this move," Secretary of the Navy Welles complained in his diary, "and without exception, I think, it struck them unfavorably that the Chief Magistrate should have gone on such a mission." Congressional Radicals, in particular, feared that the personable yet wily Stephens would bamboozle the president, parlaying Lincoln's known liberality toward the South into undeserved concessions. But that isn't what happened.

The Hampton Roads Conference began on the morning of February 3, when Stephens, Hunter, and Campbell joined Lincoln and Seward aboard the *River Queen*. Several days later, Lincoln prepared a report for Congress that revealed very little of what was said during their four-hour conversation. The peace commissioners avoided the question of reunion, Lincoln wrote, wanting to arrange an armistice first—"which, as some of them seemed to argue, might or might not lead to reunion, but which course, we

The side-wheeler *River Queen* tied up alongside a wharf. After the war, the steamboat became a ferry, serving Martha's Vineyard and Nantucket.

thought, would amount to an indefinite postponement [of reunion]. The conference ended without result."

After the war, however, all three Confederate participants published extended narratives of the conference in magazines and memoirs. These recollections have allowed historians to piece together a more detailed, if somewhat one-sided, account of what took place.

Lincoln and Stephens began the meeting by greeting one another warmly. Having served together in Congress during the 1840s and having worked together on Zachary Taylor's 1848 presidential campaign, the two of them took a few moments to reminisce about their days as Whig allies. The exchange set a friendly tone that lasted the entire day.

Stephens then segued to the matter at hand, asking Lincoln, "Well, Mr. President, is there no way of putting an end to the present trouble, and bringing about a restoration of the general good feeling and harmony *then* existing between the different States and Sections of the country?" Lincoln replied simply that he knew of only one way: for those resisting the national authority to cease their resistance. "But, said I, is there no other question that might divert the attention of both Parties, for a time, from the questions involved in their present strife, until the passions on both sides might cool?" Recognizing Stephens' allusion to Blair's quixotic Mexican proposal, Lincoln quickly moved to distance himself from Blair's conversation with

TO my remarks he [Lincoln] responded in a cheerful and cordial manner, as if the remembrance of those times, and our connection with the incidents referred to, had awakened in him a train of agreeable reflections, extending to others. Mutual inquiries were made after the fate and wellbeing of several who had been our intimate friends and active associates in a "Congressional Taylor Club," well known at the time. I inquired especially after Mr. Truman Smith of Connecticut, and he after Mr. [Robert] Toombs, William Ballard Preston, Thomas S. Flournoy, and others.

—ALEXANDER H. STEPHENS
*A Constitutional View of the Late War
between the States* (1870)

Davis. "The restoration of the Union is a sine qua non with me, and hence my instructions that no conference was to be held except upon that basis," he told Stephens emphatically. Lincoln then went on to explain, equally bluntly, that he could "entertain no proposition for ceasing active military operations which was not based upon a pledge first given for the ultimate restoration of the Union."

Because the Confederate commissioners had no authority to give such a pledge, the conversation reached an impasse, and the participants fell silent for a time. Then Campbell spoke up. Given the Southerners' agreement to Lincoln's terms, he asked, how would such reunion take place? That is, how would the practical details be worked out? How would the legalities be handled?

According to Stephens, this line of questioning had been prearranged. The commissioners had agreed in advance, Stephens wrote, "that if we failed in securing an Armistice, we would then endeavor to ascertain on what terms the Administration at Washington would be willing to end the war."

Restoration would be simple, Lincoln answered. The Southern states need only disband their armies and accept the resumption of federal authority. All other issues would be settled by the courts and by Congress.

Not surprisingly, this answer didn't satisfy Campbell, whose legal mind was quite penetrating. The war, he countered, had given rise to numerous matters of law that "required stipulation or agreement of some sort" before restoration could be achieved. As an example, the former Supreme Court justice cited the confiscation of private property by both sides. Having been seized and sold, it could hardly now be returned.

From private property to slavery was but a small step; and when Seward suggested that Congress "would no doubt be liberal in making restitution of confiscated property," Stephens asked directly what would become of the Southern slave population. Would the whole be emancipated, or only that portion which had come under Union control?

According to Stephens, Lincoln replied that emancipation would become "a judicial question." Once the war ended and his war powers ceased, the Emancipation Proclamation would become "inoperative," the president explained. The courts would then have to decide who was free and who wasn't. He personally believed they would hold that the proclamation applied only to those slaves who had passed to Union control. "But," he acknowledged, "the Courts might decide the other way, and hold that it effectively emancipated all the slaves."

At this point, Seward revealed to the Confederates that while Grant had detained them at City Point, Congress had passed an antislavery amendment. It was "a war measure," the secretary of state said, like the Emancipation Proclamation. If the war ceased immediately and the Southern states returned to the Union, Seward continued, the amendment probably wouldn't be ratified. Then, to make his point even more clear, Seward and the commissioners went through the math: thirty-six states in the Union, twenty-seven required to ratify, and therefore only ten needed to block. As they all knew, there were eleven states in the Confederacy.

According to Stephens' account, Lincoln never disputed Seward's implication that the amendment lacked popular support in the North and might be reversible. Instead, after a thoughtful silence, his head bowed in deep reflection, the president offered this suggestion:

Stephens, if I were in Georgia, and entertained the sentiments I do—though, I suppose, I should not be permitted to stay there long with them; but if I resided in Georgia, with my present sentiments,

I'll tell you what I would do, if I were in your place: I would go home and get the Governor of the State to call the Legislature together, and get them to recall all the State troops from the war; elect Senators and Members to Congress, and ratify this Constitutional Amendment prospectively, so as to take effect—say in five years. Such a ratification would be valid in my opinion. I have looked into the subject, and think such a prospective ratification would be valid. Whatever may have been the views of your people before the war, they must be convinced now, that Slavery is doomed. It cannot last long in any event, and the best course, it seems to me, for your public men to pursue, would be to adopt such a policy as will avoid, as far as possible, the evils of immediate emancipation. This would be my course, if I were in your place.

Reviving in this way his own long-standing preference for gradual, compensated emancipation, Lincoln went on to say that he would be willing to remunerate Southerners if they abolished slavery voluntarily. According to Stephens, Lincoln remarked that "he knew some who were in favor of an appropriation as high as Four Hundred Million Dollars for this purpose. I could mention persons, said he, whose names would astonish you, who are willing to do this, if the war shall now cease without further expense, and with the abolition of slavery as stated."

Thus ended the conference. Stephens, Hunter, and Campbell returned to the *Mary Martin* for their journey back up the James to Richmond, while Lincoln and Seward made for Annapolis aboard the *River Queen*, arriving shortly before dawn and quickly continuing on to Washington amid intense public speculation. During the day, however, special editions of nearly every newspaper informed readers that nothing had happened. "The conference occupied four hours," the *New York Times* reported, "and is positively known to have resulted in no change of attitude, either of the Government or of the rebels. In other words it was a failure."

A page from Lincoln's February 10 report to Congress on the Hampton Roads Conference. The document mostly contained copies of relevant correspondence.

Lincoln would not have agreed. Although peace had not been achieved, the peace issue, it seemed, had finally been put to rest. The Hampton Roads Conference, the *New York Times* editorialized a few days later, "made unmistakably clear the exact position of the contending

President Lincoln (standing at the podium) delivers his second inaugural address on the east steps of the Capitol.

parties . . . that the South is fighting for independence, and that only by successful war on our part can the Union be maintained. The demonstration thus afforded of this fact ought to unite all men, without distinction of party, in a cordial support of the Government and a vigorous prosecution of the war." Meanwhile, in Congress, members of both parties concluded (from the little they knew) that the president had handled the Confederates magnificently, hearing them out yet standing firm on the Union war aims. The North hadn't known such political unity since the start of the war.

Lincoln's give-'em-enough-rope strategy had prevailed, but to suggest that the headiness of the venture hadn't unsettled him is to give a misleading impression. In fact, the president was affected more than anyone

realized; and for a short time afterward, he had difficulty maintaining his bearings. Most notably, he came to believe briefly that the liberality he had displayed at Hampton Roads would persuade Southerners, if not the Confederate administration, to end the war now rather than push on to ultimate defeat. To that end, on February 5, he presented to his cabinet a proposal to issue four hundred million dollars' worth of government bonds. The bonds would be used to compensate Southern slaveholders. Half of the money would be paid if all armed resistance ceased by April 1. The other half would be paid if the Thirteenth Amendment was ratified by July 1. The stunned cabinet immediately expressed its unanimous disapproval, and the matter was dropped. The war, of course, went on.

The grand reception that the Lincolns hosted at the White House following the president's second inauguration.

THERE was a Cabinet meeting last evening. The President had matured a scheme which he hoped would be successful in promoting peace. It was a proposition for paying the expenses of the war for two hundred days, or four hundred millions, to the Rebel States, to be for the extinguishment of slavery, or for such purpose as the States were disposed. This in few words was the scheme. It did not meet with favor, but was dropped. The earnest desire of the President to conciliate and effect peace was manifest, but there may be such a thing as so overdoing as to cause a distrust or adverse feeling. In the present temper of Congress the proposed measure, if a wise one, could not be carried through successfully.

—**GIDEON WELLES**
(Diary entry, February 6, 1865)

THE fall of Fort Fisher in early 1865 was a heavy blow to the Confederacy. Since 1861, the fort's massive batteries had kept Union warships at bay, protecting British blockade runners as they passed into and out of Wilmington, North Carolina, the South's main Atlantic port. The capture of the fort on January 15, followed five weeks later by the fall of Wilmington itself, cut off the Rebels' last major trade route and with it the foreign food, clothing, and munitions that supplied Lee's army. To shrewd observers in the North and South alike, the final defeat of the Confederacy seemed not far off.

On March 3, the day before Lincoln's second inauguration, Stanton passed on to the president an important telegram from Grant. The previous day, the general had received a letter from Lee proposing settlement talks. Lee had inferred Grant's willingness to talk from a meeting between Longstreet and Ord, held with Grant's leave, to discuss Longstreet's request for a prisoner exchange. Lee wrote:

Lieut. Gen. Longstreet has informed me that in a recent conversation between himself and Maj. Gen. Ord as to the possibility of arriving at a satisfactory adjustment of the present unhappy difficulties by means of a military convention, Gen. Ord stated that if I desired to have an interview with you on the subject you would not decline, provided I had authority to act. Sincerely desiring to leave nothing untried which may put an end to the calamities of war, I propose to meet you at such convenient time and place as you may designate with the hope that upon an interchange of views it may be found practicable to submit the subjects of controversy between belligerents to a convention of the kind mentioned.

Responding to Grant's request for direction, Lincoln wrote out a telegram to be sent in Stanton's name so as to respect the proper chain of command. Under no circumstances, the president ordered, should Grant meet with Lee "unless it be for the capitulation of Gen. Lee's army, or on some minor, and purely, military matter." Furthermore, Grant was "not to decide, discuss, or confer upon any political question. Such questions the President holds in his own hands; and will submit them to no military conferences or conventions. Meantime you are to press to the utmost, your military advantages."

By this time, Grant's advantages were many. He had amassed 130,000 troops in and around Petersburg, compared to 50,000 for Lee. All the Federals had to do was shake the Rebels loose from their strong entrenchments. Once out in the open, the Army of Northern Virginia could be destroyed and Richmond taken. Grant just had to wait for the spring rains to pass and the muddy ground to harden. Then he could bring the interminable ten-month siege of Petersburg to an end. Meanwhile, Sherman, who had marched up from Georgia, was bringing 80,000 men to bear against Joseph Johnston's 40,000 in North Carolina. As Lincoln described the situation to a White House visitor, "Grant has the bear by the hind leg while Sherman takes off the hide."

The March 20, 1865, telegram that Grant sent to Lincoln inviting the president to visit City Point.

ONE of the most anxious periods of my experience during the rebellion was the last few weeks before [the final assault on] Petersburg. I felt that the situation of the Confederate army was such that they would try to make an escape at the earliest practicable moment, and I was afraid, every morning, that I would awake from my sleep to hear that Lee had gone, and that nothing was left but a picket line. He had his railroad by the way of Danville south, and I was afraid that he was running off his men and all stores and ordnance except such as it would be necessary to carry with him for his immediate defense. I knew he could move much more lightly and more rapidly than I, and that, if he got the start, he would leave me behind so that we would have the same army to fight again farther south—and the war might be prolonged another year.

—ULYSSES S. GRANT
Personal Memoirs (1885–86)

On March 20, with the final phase of the war approaching, Grant invited Lincoln to join him at the front. "Can you not visit City Point for a day or two?" Grant wrote. "I would like very much to see you, and I think the rest would do you good." Lincoln wasn't sleeping much at this point in his presidency, and the pressures of wartime office, Grant knew, were bearing down on him harder than ever. But the general had a more pressing reason to seek Lincoln's company: he wanted to discuss personally with the president what terms of surrender to offer Lee.

For his part, Lincoln welcomed the opportunity to get away from the press of petitioners and duties at the White House. With the help of Assistant Secretary of the Navy Gustavus Fox, he arranged passage to City Point aboard the *Bat*, a small but well-armed dispatch boat. He planned to travel alone and stay about a week, but this didn't sit well with Mary Lincoln. Not wanting to be separated for so long, she decided to accompany him on the journey.

On March 21, Lincoln summoned Lt. Comdr. John S. Barnes, captain of the *Bat*, to his office, where he informed Barnes of the change in plans. "Mr. Lincoln received me with great cordiality, but with a certain kind of embarrassment, and a look of sadness which rather embarrassed me," Barnes recalled. "After a few casual remarks, he said that Mrs. Lincoln had decided that she would accompany him to City Point—could the *Bat* accommodate her and

This photograph from 1864 shows Union soldiers in one of the trenches around Petersburg during the siege.

her maidservant?" An understandably uncomfortable Barnes tried to explain, as politely as he could, that the *Bat* was not "adapted to the private life of womankind" and could not be made so. "Well, I understand," Lincoln said gently, "but you will have to see mother."

Barnes was then brought before Mrs. Lincoln, who received him graciously. "I am going with the President to City Point," she said, "and I want you to arrange your ship to take me, my maid and my officer [personal body-guard], as well as the President." Knowing he wouldn't be able to comply, Barnes turned to Fox, who agreed that the *Bat* could never be made suitable for the first lady. Together, they went to see a sympathetic Lincoln, who joked with them about the problem but declined to get involved. In the end, Fox decided that the Lincolns would travel instead aboard the unarmed but better appointed *River Queen*, with the *Bat* acting as an escort. The convoy departed the Sixth Street Wharf at 1 P.M. on March 23,

arriving at the City Point dock (within walking distance of Grant's headquarters) at 9 P.M. the following evening.

Although the hour was late, Grant boarded the *River Queen* soon after its arrival to inform the president that he expected a Confederate attack at any moment. Rebel desertions had been growing in recent days, Grant explained, indicating that Lee's time was running short. If the Confederate commander intended to rendezvous with Johnston's army in North Carolina (which Grant thought likely), he would have to make the attempt soon, before losing any more manpower.

The attack predicted by Grant came seven hours later on the northeast end of the Union lines near Fort Steadman. At 3 A.M. on March 25, Southerners began emerging from the darkness, pretending to be deserters. Actually, they were saboteurs, deployed in advance of an assault force led by Maj. Gen. John B. Gordon. About 4 A.M., Gordon's three divisions struck—surprising the

This 1864 drawing shows the military railroad constructed by the Union to service the front at Petersburg.

Federals, capturing Fort Steadman, and punching a hole in the Union line three-quarters of a mile wide. But Lee's depleted army lacked the strength to exploit these gains, and gradually Gordon's attack lost momentum. When the stunned Federals finally rallied, Gordon had to fall back. By 7:30 A.M., Grant's troops had recaptured Fort Steadman and restored the line.

The Lincolns' eldest son, Robert, then a captain attached to Grant's staff, joined his parents for breakfast that morning. As they ate, Robert briefed his father on the action at Fort Steadman. Intrigued, Lincoln passed word to Grant that he would like to visit the battlefield. At first, Grant refused, not wanting to endanger the president by exposing him to possible enemy fire. However, when later reports indicated that the area was secure, he relented and permitted Lincoln to ride the bumpy military railroad up to the front.

The decisive phase of the battle, in which Union troops turned back Gordon's men in gruesome hand-to-hand fighting, had taken place along a short stretch of railroad embankment. The president's coach stopped at this point. Dead and wounded soldiers clogged the ground around the train. As burial parties attended to the corpses, surgeons treated the wounded they could save, while members of the Sanitary Commission distributed food and water. Lincoln looked on in awe. He had been to battlefields before, of course, but never in the immediate aftermath of combat.

According to Barnes, who accompanied the president to the front, "Mr. Lincoln was quiet and observant, making few comments, and listened to explanations in a cool, collected manner, betraying no excitement; but his whole face showed sympathetic feeling for the scene before him." On their return trip to City Point, a noticeably drained Lincoln remarked to Barnes that "he had seen enough of the horrors of war, that he hoped this was the beginning of the end, and that there would be no more bloodshed."

Back at Grant's headquarters, a seemingly revived

Lincoln sat for a time by the campfire, entertaining the general and his staff with some of the humorous fron tier anecdotes for which he was justly famous. With these men—and with Grant, in par-ticular—Lincoln could share the awful burden of authority over life and death. As they sat together, talking, Grant and Lincoln tried to glimpse the shape of things to come. They also looked forward to the day when they could each shed the immense personal power that neither enjoyed wielding.

Two days later, Lincoln and Grant met with Sherman, just arrived from North Carolina, and Rear Adm. David Dixon Porter aboard the *River Queen*. Their conversation was easygoing, mostly devoted to social pleasantries and Sherman's report on the progress of his campaign. The next day, the four men reconvened aboard the *River Queen*, this time to discuss the more portentous matter that had brought Lincoln and Sherman to City Point: what was to be done with the defeated Rebel armies?

Grant began by informing the president that, as they spoke, Maj. Gen. Philip H. Sheridan was leading a large force of cavalry, supported by two corps of infantry, across the James River via a pontoon bridge. Sheridan's purpose was to overrun the South Side Railroad near a strategic

Grant (second from left) relaxes with members of his staff at his headquarters in City Point, Virginia.

crossroads known as Five Forks. This, Grant explained, would cut off the Rebels' last major supply line and bring Lee's situation "to a crisis." If the Confederate commander chose to remain in Richmond, Grant would starve him out; if he tried to escape to North Carolina, Grant would give chase and, with Sherman's help, destroy the Army of Northern Virginia there. Sherman agreed that his forces were strong enough to take on the combined might of Lee and Johnston, provided that Grant showed up within a day or two.

At this point, Sherman asked Lincoln bluntly whether he was prepared for the imminent defeat of the Confederacy. Had the president considered what should be done with the defeated Rebel soldiers? Had he given any thought to the Confederate leadership? For example, should Jefferson Davis be permitted to flee? Certainly, it would be much easier politically to let Davis escape to Mexico or

BOTH General Grant and myself supposed that one or the other of us would have to fight one more bloody battle, and that it would be the last. Mr. Lincoln exclaimed, more than once, that there had been blood enough shed, and asked us if another battle could not be avoided. I remember well to have said that we could not control that event; that this necessarily rested with our enemy, and I inferred that both Jeff. Davis and General Lee would be forced to fight one more desperate and bloody battle.

—**WILLIAM T. SHERMAN**
Memoirs of General William T. Sherman (1875)

G. P. A. Healy's 1868 painting *The Peacemakers* shows General Sherman (left), General Grant (second from left), and Admiral Porter (right) meeting with President Lincoln aboard the *River Queen* in late March 1865.

the lemonade would be much more palatable if he added a little brandy. The man said he wouldn't object so long as his friend added the brandy "unbeknown to him." From this story, Grant and Sherman inferred that Lincoln wouldn't object to Jefferson Davis' escape so long as the escape could be accomplished "unbeknown to him."

ROBERT E. Lee had never been an eager combatant. "This is the people's war," he liked to say when compelled to address soldiers who had shirked their duty; "when they tire, I stop." By the spring of 1865, "the people" had clearly tired of the war, and Lee knew that the end was near, but still he couldn't stop. His sense of duty overwhelmed him. He was trapped.

On March 26, the day after the failure at Fort Steadman, Lee wrote to Davis, "I fear now it will be impossible to prevent a junction between Grant and Sherman, nor do I deem it prudent that this army should maintain its position until the latter shall approach too near." Lee then presented Davis with some arithmetic. Desertions had

Canada than to put him on trial for treason.

Lincoln assured Sherman that he was prepared. "All he wanted of us," Sherman recalled, "was to defeat the opposing armies, and to get the men composing the Confederate armies back to their homes, at work on their farms and in their shops. As to Jeff. Davis, he was hardly at liberty to speak his mind fully, but intimated that he ought to clear out, 'escape the county,' only it would not do for him to say so openly."

To illustrate the point, Lincoln told a story about a man who had pledged total abstinence from liquor. One day, while visiting a friend, he was offered a drink. Citing his pledge, the man declined. His friend then offered him a lemonade, which he gratefully accepted. While preparing the lemonade, the friend pointed to a bottle of liquor and remarked that

AFTER sending my note this morning, I received from the express office a bag of socks. You will have to send down your offerings as soon as you can, and bring your work to a close, for I think General Grant will move against us soon—within a week, if nothing prevents—and no man can tell what may be the result; but trusting to a merciful God, who does not always give the battle to the strong, I pray we may not be overwhelmed. I shall, however, endeavour to do my duty and fight to the last. Should it be necessary to abandon our position to prevent being surrounded, what will you do? You must consider the question, and make up your mind. It is a fearful condition, and we must rely for guidance and protection upon a kind Providence.

—**ROBERT E. LEE**
(Letter to his wife, February 21, 1865)

Mathew Brady created this portrait of Robert E. Lee on April 16, 1865, the general's first full day at home in Richmond after his return from Appomattox.

reduced Johnston's army in North Carolina to just 13,500 infantry. At that strength, Johnston couldn't possibly resist Sherman, whose own strength Johnston estimated at 60,000. Meanwhile, Grant, in Lee's judgment, had between 80,000 and 100,000 men. "Their two armies united," Lee explained to Davis, "would therefore exceed ours by nearly one hundred thousand." The only hope for the Confederates in Richmond, Lee concluded, was to evacuate the city as soon as possible.

Unfortunately, practical and psychological constraints slowed

Confederate soldiers captured at Five Forks being led to the rear by Union guards.

the Rebels' departure. On the practical side, the roads were still muddy, Gordon's men needed a day or so to recover, and the transfer of supplies had to be organized. On the psychological side, the civil administration was in disarray. Unwilling to accept that the "dreaded contingency" might ever arise, Davis had eschewed all preparation, and so there was chaos. While Lee surveyed his ordnance stores, prepared maps for the retreat, and strengthened his extreme right flank—against which he believed (correctly) Grant's attack would shortly come—Davis scrambled to assemble his administration's most important papers and move the government to Danville, the next Confederate capital.

On Friday, March 31, Sheridan, now in position, made ready to strike. With Richmond still not fully prepared for evacuation, Lee ordered Maj. Gen. George E. Pickett to "Hold Five Forks at all hazards." However, even with the reinforcements Lee had sent, this proved impossible. Sheridan captured the crossroads on April 1, and Lee began evacuating the city the next day, sooner than he would have liked. "This is a sad business, colonel," Lee remarked to an aide. "It has happened as I told them in Richmond it would happen. The line has been stretched until it is broken."

On the night of April 2, explosions rocked the Confederate capital—caused not by Northern artillery, but by Southerners detonating large stockpiles of ammunition that couldn't be transported. Early the next morning, with the Rebels gone but explosions and fires still alarming the city, the residents of Richmond experienced an even

Dennis Malone Carter's 1866 painting *Lincoln's Drive Through Richmond* depicts the president's April 4 tour of the captured Confederate capital. Although blacks welcomed Lincoln enthusiastically, most whites turned away from his carriage.

greater shock: the sight of the first Union troops entering the capital. They weren't just Federals; they were blacks, members of the Fifth Massachusetts Colored Cavalry and Twenty-ninth Connecticut Colored Infantry. "Thus another link in the chain of anarchy and degradation has been severed," one of these soldiers later wrote.

A day later, on the morning of April 4, Lincoln traveled up the James on the *River Queen*. After transferring briefly to the warship *Malvern*, he was rowed ashore at Richmond by twelve sailors in a gig. At that point, escorted only by Admiral Porter, three other officers, and ten marines armed with carbines, the president walked from the river to the White House of the Confederacy, vacated by Jefferson Davis just thirty-six hours earlier. In the afternoon, Lincoln again toured the city, this time in an open carriage accompanied by a much stronger security detail.

Meanwhile, having crossed the Appomattox River on the night of April 2, Lee headed southwest toward Danville, with the Union armies of the Potomac and the James not far behind. On April 4, the Army of Northern Virginia arrived at Amelia Court House, where it expected to find a cache of fresh supplies. There were none.

Following a parallel course, Sheridan's cavalry overtook the Confederates and seized Jetersville, blocking Lee's route and forcing him to turn west toward Lynchburg. On April 6, the Confederate column became dangerously strung out in the swampy bottomland along Sailor's Creek, allowing the Federals to isolate and capture eight thousand men, or a fifth of Lee's remaining force. On the evening of April 7, Grant and Lee began exchanging messages.

"The result of the last week must convince you of the hopelessness of further resistance on the part of the Army of Northern Virginia in this struggle," Grant wrote. "I feel that it is so, and regard it as my duty to shift from myself the responsibility of any further effusion of blood by asking of you the surrender of that portion of the C. S. Army known as the Army of Northern Virginia."

"I have received your note of this date," Lee replied. "Though not entertaining the opinion you express of the hopelessness of further resistance on the part of the Army of Northern Virginia, I reciprocate your desire to avoid useless effusion of blood, and therefore, before considering your proposition, ask the terms you will offer on condition of its surrender."

On April 8, while the exchange of notes continued, elements of Ord's Army of the James outmarched the Rebels and took up a position on the Lynchburg Road, trapping Lee's army near Appomattox Court House. At dawn on April 9, Lee tried to fight his way out. When that failed, the Confederate commander had no choice but to submit.

Lee's message found its way to Grant shortly before noon. The Union commander, who had been suffering from terrible headaches, dismounted and sat down in the road to compose a reply. A few hours later, the two generals met at the Appomattox home of Wilmer McLean, where Lee accepted Grant's generous terms of surrender: all Rebels would be permitted to return home once they

The ruins of Richmond, photographed not long after the city's fall.

Generals Grant and Lee meet in the parlor of the McLean home in Appomattox Court House to arrange terms in Louis Guillaume's 1867 painting of the surrender.

disarmed and promised not to take up arms again; all officers could keep their sidearms; all cavalrymen could keep their mounts. After signing the necessary papers, Lee addressed his men: "I have done for you all that was in my power to do. You have all done your duty. Leave the result to God. Go to your homes and resume your occupations. Obey the laws and become as good citizens as you were soldiers."

LINCOLN returned to Washington at sundown on April 9. People filled the streets, still celebrating the fall of Richmond. Later that night, the president learned of Lee's surrender. At dawn on April 10, the firing of five hundred cannon announced the news to the rest of the city. "The tidings were spread over the country during the night, and the nation seems delirious with joy," Gideon Welles wrote in his diary. "Guns are firing, bells ringing, flags flying, men laughing, children cheering; all, all are jubilant. This surrender of the great Rebel captain and the most formidable and reliable army of the Secessionists virtually terminates the Rebellion. There may be some marauding, and robbing and murder by desperadoes, but no great battle, no conflict of armies, after the news of yesterday reaches the different sections."

At the White House, revelers filled the North Portico, carriageways, and sidewalks. "The crowds around the house have been immense," Mary Lincoln wrote her friend Charles Sumner. "In the midst of the bands playing, they break forth into singing." They also called for the president, shouting his name louder and louder until he finally appeared. Surprising everyone, Lincoln asked the band to play the Rebel anthem "Dixie," which it did. "I have always thought 'Dixie' one of the best tunes I have ever heard," the president joked. "Our adversaries over the way attempted to appropriate it, but I insisted yesterday that we fairly captured it. I presented the question to the Attorney General, and he gave it as his legal opinion that it is our lawful prize."

Four nights later, still in a celebratory mood, Lincoln agreed to accompany Mary to Ford's Theatre for a performance of the popular comedy *Our American Cousin*. Shortly after ten o'clock, John Wilkes Booth entered the lightly guarded presidential box and shot Lincoln in the back of the head with a .44-caliber single-bullet derringer.

Next, Booth leaped from the box to the stage. As he descended, however, his right boot spur caught the U.S. flag decorating the box. This caused him to lose his balance, land awkwardly, and break his leg. Nevertheless, he managed to make his way outside, mount his waiting horse, and flee to Virginia.

The dying Lincoln was carried across the street to the Petersen boardinghouse, where his six-foot-four-inch frame was laid diagonally across a bed in one of the empty rooms. There was little else anyone could do for him. As news of the shooting spread, members of the cabinet began to arrive at the boardinghouse to keep vigil. Never regaining consciousness, the president was pronounced dead at 7:22 the next morning. "Now he belongs to the ages," Secretary of War Stanton said.

ABOVE: The derringer used by John Wilkes Booth to assassinate
Abraham Lincoln in his box at Ford's Theatre.

TOP: This 1865 print shows the room in Petersen's boardinghouse
to which the president was carried after he was shot.

RIGHT: The manhunt for John Wilkes Booth and coconspirator
David Herold lasted twelve days, by which time all of the other
conspirators had been arrested.

VI

Reconstructing the Nation

ᘒᘓ

ALTHOUGH Lee's surrender at Appomattox brought a quick end to the military phase of the Civil War, it didn't resolve any of the legal problems raised by John Campbell at Hampton Roads. The Confederacy was defeated, but what of the Confederate states? What would their status be, and that of the freed slaves? These questions grabbed the national attention in April 1865 and held it tightly for several years.

In Washington, the legal status of the Rebel states had been a point of contention almost since the war began. Initially, President Lincoln adopted the position that the governments of the Southern states had rebelled, not the states per se. Therefore, if Southerners ceased their resistance to the national authority and established new (loyal) state governments, they could swiftly resume their place as citizens of the United States, enjoying all the rights and privileges thereto appertaining.

The problem with this theory—in addition to its failure to exact any price for secession—was that it belonged more to the antebellum world in which *United States* was a plural noun than to the emerging world of a singular nation. Recognizing this, Lincoln shaded his views as the war dragged on. In particular, he moved beyond restoration of the status quo ante bellum to insist that emancipation be part of any negotiated settlement.

Congress favored a different theoretical approach that, not coincidentally, placed Reconstruction much more firmly under its jurisdiction. Most Republican congressmen subscribed to Charles Sumner's state-suicide theory—which held that, by seceding, the Rebel states had forfeited

OPPOSITE: **Union troops parade up Pennsylvania Avenue from the Capitol during the Grand Review of the Armies on May 23–24, 1865.**

their rights as states under the Constitution and were now reduced to the status of territories. Following this logic, the Rebel states could not rejoin the Union simply by ending their resistance. Congress would have to readmit them on terms of its own choosing.

Thaddeus Stevens, the Radical leader in the House, took up an even more extreme position. The Confederate states had certainly lost their constitutional legitimacy, he agreed, but he didn't think they deserved to be treated as territories, the citizens of which had certain rights under the Constitution. Rather, he believed them to be "conquered provinces," subject only to the international law of war—which allowed conquerors to treat vanquished enemies generally as they pleased.

The political situation in April 1865 was thus difficult enough without the complicating factor of the freedpeople. What would their place in postwar society be? How would their transition from bondage to freedom be handled? In fact, what did it mean to be free in America?

LINCOLN'S first Reconstruction initiative was the Proclamation of Amnesty and Reconstruction, issued on December 8, 1863. By this time, the Union army had occupied most of southern Louisiana, and Lincoln was eager to provide a road map for the state's restoration.

The proclamation offered most Confederates amnesty if they swore an oath of allegiance to the Constitution and accepted the abolition of slavery. (A few groups were excluded, such as high-ranking military officers and government officials.) In a given state, once the number of oath-takers reached 10 percent of the number of votes cast in the 1860 presidential election, the loyal minority could draft a new state constitution and establish a new state government that Lincoln would recognize.

Although Republicans generally accepted the president's lenient Ten Percent Plan, more than a few Radicals had misgivings. On December 22, abolitionist Wendell Phillips delivered a speech at Cooper Union in New York City, criticizing the president for disregarding the needs of the freedpeople. "That proclamation frees the slave and ignores the Negro," Phillips declared. Lincoln's plan also offended Thaddeus Stevens, who had two complaints. First, the president had no competence in Reconstruction and therefore lacked the authority to offer restoration. Second, and more personally, he deplored Lincoln's willingness to forgive so easily Rebels who had caused so much harm to the nation.

Meanwhile, restoration wasn't going well in Louisiana. The "loyal" community being cultivated by the president had split into two camps: conservatives, who wanted to restore the old political order (albeit without slavery); and Radicals, who wanted to lead a class revolution against the planter aristocracy. The chief proxies in this struggle were the well-educated, economically successful free blacks of New Orleans. At the constitutional convention held under the Ten Percent Plan in the spring of 1864, the conservatives won, their profound racism on open display. Although a Negro regiment guarded the convention hall against Confederate marauders, the conservatives refused suffrage to all African Americans, including Union army veterans and quadroons. Even worse, the state government elected by whites under the new constitution restricted the rights of blacks and generally abused them.

Aware of these developments, the Radicals in Congress decided they couldn't allow the emerging pseudo-slavery in Louisiana to stand, lest it set a precedent for the rest of the reconstructed Confederacy. Urged on by Sumner and Stevens, they blocked the seating of the congressmen sent to Washington by the restored Louisiana government and set about asserting congressional control of Reconstruction in accordance with the Sumner and Stevens theories of secession. The resulting Wade-Davis Bill required not 10 percent but "a majority" of a state's 1860 voting population to swear a loyalty oath before the state could apply to Congress for readmission. Moreover, the pledge specified in the bill was the so-called ironclad oath, which required oath-takers to affirm that they "have never voluntarily borne arms against the United States . . . [and] have voluntarily given no aid, countenance, counsel, or encouragement to persons engaged in armed hostility

thereto," thereby excluding all former Confederates. The bill's Radical authors would have provided for black suffrage as well had not strong opposition persuaded Sen. Benjamin F. Wade that fighting for African-American voting rights would "sacrifice the bill."

Because Lincoln opposed the state-suicide theory, and also because he didn't want to see his efforts in Louisiana come to naught, the president pocket-vetoed the Wade-Davis Bill in July 1864. This action didn't end Radical agitation for control of Reconstruction, of course—which Montgomery Blair was quick to point out when he began lobbying for passage of the antislavery amendment five months later.

WHILE the legislative and executive branches of the federal government dueled over policy, some military commanders took practical aspects of Reconstruction into their own hands. A common problem was caring for the thousands of contrabands burdening Union armies in the field. In early 1863, Brig. Gen. Lorenzo Thomas devised a plan to lease abandoned Confederate plantations in the Mississippi Valley to Northern entrepreneurs willing to employ former slaves under labor terms set by the army. Thomas' plan gave able-bodied freedmen three choices: they could enlist in the Union army, become military laborers, or go to work on a leased plantation. The "compulsory labor" contracts they were forced to sign (or else be arrested for vagrancy) paid meager wages and bound them to their employer until the one-year term of the contract was up. Although ostensibly emancipated, these laborers weren't allowed to leave their plantations for any reason without the specific permission of their employers. To many in the North, Thomas' compulsory labor system looked a great deal like slavery.

A different labor arrangement obtained at Davis Bend, just south of Vicksburg, where the family of the Confederate president owned a large plantation. After Jefferson Davis' brother Joseph fled to Tuscaloosa in 1862, his slaves took over management of the plantation and ran it so well that General Grant, when he arrived there in 1863, decided to let them continue as lessees. (A "negro paradise," Grant called it.) After the fall of Vicksburg, the army settled more former slaves on neighboring land. Together with the original Davis family slaves, these freedpeople formed a large self-governing community that generated $160,000 in cotton profits.

This 1864 glass negative shows a group of freedpeople taking part in a wedding on the plantation at Davis Bend.

The problem of caring for tagalongs particularly burdened Sherman during his March to the Sea in late 1864. By the time he reached Savannah on December 21, some twenty thousand slaves had abandoned their masters to follow his army. On January 12, at the urging of Secretary of War Stanton, who had joined Sherman in Savannah, the general sought the advice of local black churchmen, most of them former slaves. Their spokesman, a Baptist minister named Garrison Frazier, had been held in bondage for sixty years before purchasing his freedom in 1857. When asked to "state what you understand by slavery and the freedom that was to be given by the president's [emancipation] proclamation," Frazier said:

Slavery is receiving by irresistible power the work of another man, and not by his consent. The freedom, as I understand it, promised by the proclamation, is taking us from under the yoke of bondage, and placing us where we could reap the fruit of our own labor, take care of ourselves, and assist the Government in maintaining our freedom.

Stanton and Sherman then asked Frazier how such freedom could best be accomplished. "The way we can best take care of ourselves," Frazier replied, "is to have land, and turn it and till it by our own labor."

Sherman was not a Radical. His only goal was to rid his army of the trailing slaves; but if he could do that and punish Rebel planters at the same time, so much the better. A social revolution was not what he had in mind, but that is nevertheless what he wrought.

Four days after his meeting with the churchmen, Sherman issued Special Field Order No. 15, which set aside a large area of land along the coasts of South Carolina and Georgia (including the Sea Islands) for the exclusive settlement of African-American families on forty-acre plots.

This drawing from late December 1864 shows the entrance hall of the home of Charles Green, which Sherman used as his headquarters in Savannah.

Mr. HUNTER said something about the inhumanity of leaving so many poor old negroes and young children destitute, by encouraging the able-bodied negroes to run away, and asked what are they—the helpless—to do?

Mr. LINCOLN said that reminded him of an old friend in Illinois, who had a crop of potatoes and did not want to dig them. So he told a neighbor that he would turn in his hogs and let them dig them for themselves. But, said the neighbor, the frost will soon be in the ground, and when the soil is hard frozen, what will they do then? To which the worthy farmer replied, "let 'em root!"

Mr. STEPHENS said he supposed that was the original of "Root Hog or Die," and a fair indication of the future of the negroes.

Because Sherman also offered the freedpeople fatigued mules that his army could no longer use, the phrase *forty acres and a mule* became synonymous with the general's liberal approach to Reconstruction. Although Sherman's order went well beyond anything Lincoln had proposed, the president allowed it to stand; and by June 1865, forty thousand freedpeople had settled four hundred thousand acres of "Sherman land."

HAGIOGRAPHERS who wish to claim for Lincoln pleasingly progressive views on black civil rights often suggest that his thinking was "in flux" at the time of his assassination. They have to do this because the president's actual views on race, as preserved in the historical records, are not nearly so laudatory.

An indicative anecdote can be found in the report on the Hampton Roads Conference that the Confederate peace commissioners presented to Jefferson Davis on February 6:

We know Lincoln enjoyed this story because he repeated it to Francis B. Carpenter, who lived for six months at the White House while painting *First Reading of the Emancipation Proclamation of President Lincoln*. The story demonstrates quite clearly that Lincoln was no egalitarian. Nor did he share the Radical view that the defeat of the South and the dismantling of its slave economy should inaugurate a social and political revolution. He believed, rather, like most Northerners, that while slavery was wrong, most whites were generally superior to most blacks.

One might reasonably argue that this view was lightly held. In Illinois, Lincoln rarely encountered well-educated, well-spoken African Americans; and when he met such capable men as Frederick Douglass during his presidency, he was duly impressed. On the other hand, his persistent interest in colonization suggests that he hadn't yet reached the point of feeling comfortable living among Negroes.

Above all, however, Lincoln was a fair-minded and generous person who was willing to offer freedpeople whatever help they needed. He simply didn't believe

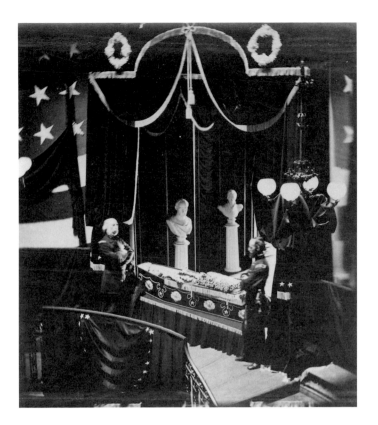

This photograph, suppressed by Secretary of War Edwin Stanton, shows President Lincoln's body lying in state in an open casket in New York's City Hall on April 24.

they would need much. In the reconstructed South, he optimistically imagined, former Whigs with repressed Unionist sympathies would step forward to resurrect the region, governing inclusively and creating prosperity for all. Lincoln even encouraged these men to grant limited black suffrage, suggesting privately to Louisiana governor Michael Hahn as early as March 1864 that at least some blacks be granted the vote "on the basis of intelligence and military service."

Vice Pres. Andrew Johnson, who succeeded Lincoln, had an altogether different mind-set. He despised the Southern plantation system but not because of slavery. He owned numerous slaves himself and had a deep, racist contempt for Negroes. Rather, he had a class hatred for the aristocratic planters who dominated the Southern economy. Having grown up poor, he identified strongly with the yeoman farmers of hardscrabble East Tennessee, who made up his political base. "Damn the Negroes," Johnson once barked at a Union general. "I am fighting those traitorous aristocrats, their masters."

THE amount of constituency, so to speak, on which the new Louisiana government rests, would be more satisfactory to all if it contained fifty, thirty, or even twenty thousand, instead of only about twelve thousand, as it does. It is also unsatisfactory to some that the elective franchise is not given to the colored man. I would myself prefer that it were now conferred on the very intelligent, and on those who serve our cause as soldiers. Still the question is not whether the Louisiana government, as it stands, is quite all that is desirable. The question is, Will it be wiser to take it as it is, and help to improve it; or to reject, and disperse it? Can Louisiana be brought into proper practical relation with the Union sooner by sustaining, or by discarding her new State Government? . . .

What has been said of Louisiana will apply generally to other States. And yet so great peculiarities pertain to each state, and such important and sudden changes occur in the same state; and withal, so new and unprecedented is the whole case, that no exclusive, and inflexible plan can be safely prescribed as to details and collaterals. Such exclusive and inflexible plan would surely become a new entanglement. Important principles may, and must, be inflexible.

In the present "situation," as the phrase goes, it may be my duty to make some new announcement to the people of the South. I am considering, and shall not fail to act, when satisfied that action will be proper.

—**ABRAHAM LINCOLN**
(Last public speech, April 11, 1865)

The Lincoln conspirators also planned to assassinate Vice Pres. Andrew Johnson (shown here in a wartime photograph) and Secretary of State William H. Seward.

Johnson was serving in the Senate when Tennessee seceded from the Union in June 1861. Every other senator from a Confederate state resigned his seat following secession. Johnson alone chose to remain loyal. In March 1862, after the Union occupied East Tennessee, Lincoln named Johnson the state's military governor.

By 1865, however, Johnson was much less interested in punishing the Confederacy. A quarter of a million Rebel soldiers—more than a fifth of the South's adult white male population—had died in the war, and the region's most important economic infrastructure had been demolished. The South had suffered enough, the new president believed, and his policies reflected both his compassion and the leniency of his predecessor. In most other respects, though, he was no Lincoln.

As a politician, Johnson was straightforward, decisive, and he knew his own mind. But he was also a loner, intolerant of criticism, disinclined to compromise, and he lacked Lincoln's sensitivity to Northern public opinion. Overall, his stubborn, combative personality made him ill suited to the demands of his new office.

AT the time of Lincoln's death, federal Reconstruction policy had reached a crossroads. The Southern slave-labor system was dead but not yet replaced. Would the new free-labor system be modeled on Thomas' compulsory labor contracts or on Grant and Sherman's land-redistribution policies? There were differing opinions. On one side, Southern planters were already working to establish a compulsory labor system as close to slavery as possible. Most believed that as long as they could retain title to the land, their former slaves would have no option but to work for them under whatever conditions they set. On the other side, the freedpeople pushed for access to land so that they could become economically independent. Lifetimes of forced, unpaid labor, they argued, entitled them to a small portion of their former owners' land.

Because the Thirty-ninth Congress wasn't scheduled to convene until December 1865, the authority to decide these matters fell to Johnson—who began the era of Presidential Reconstruction on May 29, when he issued a proclamation that followed, nearly word for word, Lincoln's Proclamation of Amnesty and Reconstruction. (The only meaningful difference was that Johnson added to the list of excluded Confederates those with over twenty thousand dollars' worth of taxable property—that is, the planters.) At the same time, also as Lincoln would have, he appointed provisional governors to summon constitutional conventions in the defeated states.

The conditions that Johnson established were the same ones Lincoln had set: the new constitutions would have to repudiate secession, abolish slavery, and abrogate the Confederate war debt. In all other matters, including suffrage, the various states

OUR negroes have a fall, a tall fall ahead of them, in my humble opinion. They will learn that freedom and independence are different things. A man may be free and yet not independent.

—SAMUEL AGNEW
(Mississippi planter, diary entry, December 15, 1865)

This image of Charleston after Sherman's army had passed through shows the devastation wrought by Union troops.

had the right to do as they pleased. Once voters approved these constitutions, states could elect representatives and resume their normal place in the Union. This had been Lincoln's intention, Northerners knew—to focus on reconciliation rather than vengeance—so most were willing to give Johnson's plan a try.

But the whites who came to power under this arrangement were neither the Unionist Whigs Lincoln expected nor the yeoman farmers Johnson preferred. Rather, they were the same planter elite that had brought on the war in the first place. The laws these men passed were clearly intended to re-create, as much as possible given abolition, the status quo ante bellum. Most egregious were the Black Codes, which legislated white political dominance and kept freedpeople tied to plantations by defining their "rights" in highly limited ways. For example, the Black Codes required African-American men to sign compulsory labor contracts or else be declared vagrants—a status that entitled the state to arrest, fine, and hire them out to white landowners. Texas even criminalized the use of offensive language by a Negro in the presence of his employer, his employer's agents, or his employer's family.

ABOVE: This December 1865 cartoon shows the clerk of the House refusing to seat a new Southern congressman.

BELOW: Students standing outside a school established by the Freedmen's Bureau on Edisto Island, South Carolina.

No doubt Lincoln expected some of this and would have been prepared to intervene before Northern opinion turned firmly against his Reconstruction policy. But Johnson possessed no such political skill. Instead, he contributed to the problem by compounding the inequity. During the summer of 1865, he began ordering the return of confiscated land to its former owners—including land distributed under Sherman's Special Order No. 15. Up and down the coasts of South Carolina and Georgia, freedpeople were forcibly evicted from their new homes. The experience left these people with a deep sense of betrayal that persisted in their descendants well into the twentieth century.

The evictions also outraged Radical Republicans, who were already quite upset. They deplored the resurrection of Rebel leadership, detested the Black Codes, and denounced Johnson for ignoring the rights of the freedpeople. Frequent newspaper reports of violence in the South against former slaves and Northern visitors only heightened the Radicals' indignation.

When the Thirty-ninth Congress finally convened its first session on December 4, 1865, Johnson informed it matter-of-factly that all of the Southern states had complied

with his proclamation and dutifully established loyal state governments. Therefore, "the work of restoration" was over, except "for the [ex-Confederate] States whose powers have been so long in abeyance to resume their places in the two branches of the National Legislature."

Not so fast, responded the Republicans, who now dominated both the House and the Senate. Conservatives, moderates, and Radicals alike were so unhappy with the Johnson state governments that they voted nearly unanimously to block the seating of the new Southern delegations. Meanwhile, they established a Joint Committee on Reconstruction to investigate conditions in the South and make recommendations for reform. Thaddeus Stevens was made a member of this committee but not Charles Sumner, who was considered "too ultra" by the moderates in the majority.

Led by Lyman Trumbull, the moderates subsequently introduced two bills to repair the damage (rather than start over, as the Radicals wanted). The first extended the life of the Freedmen's Bureau, established in March 1865 to ease the transition from slavery to freedom. The second (and more important) was a landmark civil rights bill that overturned *Dred Scott* by defining all people born in the United States (except Indians) as citizens. The bill also delineated specific rights to which all U.S. citizens were entitled—including "full and equal benefit of all laws and proceedings for the security of person and property as is enjoyed by white citizens," but not the right to vote. In Trumbull's words, the legislation attempted to define "what slavery is and what liberty is."

By this time, most moderates had come to accept the Radical view that the freedpeople were entitled to equality before the law—enforced, if necessary, by the newly expanded authority of the federal government. Yet the Civil Rights Bill was by no means a Radical coup. It left all of the Johnson state governments in place and merely required them to grant all citizens, black and white, the same legal rights.

Embraced by nearly all Republicans as sensible compromises with the president's positions, the two bills were passed by overwhelming majorities in both houses of Congress. Nevertheless, Johnson vetoed one and then the other on the grounds that they violated states' rights by concentrating too much power in the federal government. The president's March 27, 1866, veto of the Civil Rights Bill was especially galling to Republicans, and his mulish

THE CRUEL UNCLE AND THE VETOED BABES IN THE WOOD.

This 1866 cartoon portrays President Johnson as a "cruel uncle" leading the babes Civil Rights and Freedmen's Bureau into the Veto Wood.

refusal to give on any point pushed the moderates even farther into the Radical camp.

A confrontation became inevitable; and on April 9, the first anniversary of Lee's surrender, Congress voted to override the president's veto. (It was the first time in U.S. history that a major piece of legislation was enacted over a presidential veto.) Next, Congress moved to secure the fruits of victory in the Civil War by placing them beyond the reach of shifting electoral majorities. It did this in the same way it had secured abolition—that is, by passing another constitutional amendment, the second in sixteen months after a hiatus of sixty-one years.

The Fourteenth Amendment was approved by the Senate, 33–11, on June 8 and by the House, 120–32, on June 13. It had five sections, three of which have little relevance today. (Sections 2–4 concerned, respectively, reductions in the congressional representation of states that fail to practice universal manhood suffrage, the barring from public office of Rebels who had taken a constitutional oath, and the abrogation of the Confederate war debt.) Section 5 was a pro forma clause empowering Congress to enforce the previous four sections. Section 1, however, proved to be one of the most important and lasting developments in

American legislative history. Known as the "equal protection clause," it reads:

> *All persons born or naturalized in the United States, and subject to the jurisdiction thereof, are citizens of the United States and of the state wherein they reside. No state shall make or enforce any law which shall abridge the privileges or immunities of citizens of the United States; nor shall any state deprive any person of life, liberty, or property, without due process of law; nor deny to any person within its jurisdiction the equal protection of the laws.*

Ironically, reactionary Supreme Courts initially interpreted Section 1 of the Fourteenth Amendment to justify all manner of discrimination, including the "separate but equal" doctrine found constitutional in *Plessy v. Ferguson* (1896). As the Court became more progressive during the early twentieth century, however, its interpretation evolved. Ultimately, by midcentury, it came to embrace Section I as the basis of a new "rights revolution." Decisions such as *Brown v. Board of Education* (1954), *Gideon v.*

In this 1866 cartoon, Andrew Johnson (left) says, "Look here! One of us has got to back." Thaddeus Stevens replies, "Well, it ain't me that's going to do it—you bet!"

Wainwright (1963), *Griswold v. Connecticut* (1965), and *Miranda v. Arizona* (1966) responded, of course, to social transformations then taking place in post–World War II America; but to establish the soundness of these decisions in law, the Court referenced the Reconstruction era, when lawmakers had first dared to challenge the framers' intent.

AS expected, President Johnson opposed ratification of the Fourteenth Amendment, and his encouragement of Southern rejection drove the 1866 midterm campaign. To rally support for the conservative Republicans and Democrats who endorsed his position, he undertook an unprecedented speaking tour of the North, known as the Swing Around the Circle. There was certainly support to be had, but the president conducted himself so poorly that the effort backfired. Johnson called for reconciliation between North and South, but the manner in which he spoke was so wildly intemperate that he made the most extreme Radicals (whom he accused of plotting his assassination) seem moderate in comparison. The result was an anti-Johnson landslide, even greater Republican dominance in Congress, and a clear popular mandate for Radical Reconstruction.

When the Thirty-ninth Congress reconvened in December 1866, for its final session, Republican congressman James W. Grimes of Iowa, who had spent most of the previous session searching futilely for common ground with Johnson, gave up. "The President has no power to control or influence anybody," Grimes observed, "and legislation will be carried on entirely regardless of his opinions or wishes." The opportunity for social and political revolution longed for by the Radicals had finally arrived.

Seizing the initiative, Stevens introduced a bill requiring states restored under Presidential Reconstruction to hold new constitutional conventions, the delegates to which would be chosen by a fundamentally different electorate. This time, former Confederates would be temporarily excluded (for five years), while black men would be included. Soon afterward, because Stevens' bill didn't address the plight of the freedpeople directly, a second bill was introduced to place the South under military rule.

Two months of wrangling followed as the Republican caucus debated moderate objections to the Radical plan, such as its failure to define specific conditions for re-admission. On the whole, however, most moderates had already accepted the basic tenets of the Radical position.

Blanche K. Bruce of Mississippi served in the Senate from 1875, when federal troops still enforced black civil rights, until 1881, by which time Reconstruction had ended.

They agreed that the Johnson state governments, by enacting the Black Codes and rejecting the Fourteenth Amendment, had thoroughly discredited themselves; and they also agreed that the only course left was to establish new state governments with the direct participation of the freedpeople. On March 2, 1867, having worked out the details, Congress passed the First Reconstruction Act. Johnson immediately vetoed the bill, but by the end of the day Congress had voted to override.

The new law divided the former Confederacy into five military districts, empowering the commander of each to use U.S. Army troops as necessary "to protect all persons in their rights of person and property." (Tennessee, having been readmitted by Congress soon after its July 1866 ratification of the Fourteenth Amendment, was exempted from military rule.) The act also specified the steps a state would have to take to gain readmission. These were generally the same steps that Stevens had outlined in his original bill. In particular, the act required states to adopt universal manhood suffrage and ratify the Fourteenth Amendment before they could be readmitted. A follow-up measure—passed March 23, again over Johnson's veto—authorized the district commanders to register eligible voters and hold new elections.

Over the next several years, the presence of Northern troops permitted the establishment of genuinely interracial state governments in the South. By July 1870, all of the former Confederate states had been readmitted to the Union, and their representatives seated in Congress. But the story of Radical Reconstruction doesn't have a happy ending. Because nearly all of the white South wasn't yet ready for black membership in the body politic, the backlash was strong and irresistible. Banding together in fraternal organizations such as the Ku Klux Klan, angry whites terrorized blacks and any Unionist whites who dared to visit the polls. They also attacked the Republican party infrastructure, beating and even assassinating local leaders and elected officials.

Congress responded with the Force Act of 1870 and the Ku Klux Klan Act of 1871. These and other measures authorized President Grant (who had replaced Johnson in March 1869) to use force in defense of Southern voting rights; and Grant did his best, even placing nine South Carolina counties under martial law in October 1871. But Southern resistance to Radical Reconstruction was too persistent, too organized, too widespread, and far too violent for Grant to succeed. Meanwhile, the conflict gave

This 1872 engraving shows members of the Ku Klux Klan in disguise. Klansmen didn't adopt white robes and pointed hoods until the Klan's revival in the 1910s.

"Shall we call home our troops?" asks this January 1875 *Harper's Weekly* cartoon, which suggests that the federal government has not yet fulfilled its promises to the Negro.

Northerners pause. How willing were they, really, to fight Southerners again over the political rights of Negroes? Not very willing at all, it turned out.

By 1876, there was little Northern support left for an ongoing military presence in the South. When that year's presidential election produced a stalemate, neither candidate receiving an electoral majority, the end of Reconstruction was at hand. A special commission was appointed to decide the election. Voting strictly along party lines, the commission awarded all nineteen disputed votes to the Republican candidate, Rutherford B. Hayes of Ohio, giving him the presidency. Irate Southern Democrats, charging (with a good deal of justification) that the election had been stolen, threatened another rebellion. So, a political deal was struck. Hayes would become president; but upon taking office, he would immediately remove all federal troops from the South.

In the absence of any power to stop them, Democrats quickly chased the last remaining Republicans from office and began constructing the system of racial segregation and subjugation known as Jim Crow. A century would pass before interracial democracy returned to the South.

DESPITE its initial promise, Radical Reconstruction ended in disaster for the freedpeople because revolutions imposed from without typically produce counterrevolutions that make matters even worse. That is, because the Radicals forced so many new ideas on the South so quickly, the backlash was such that the freedpeople ended up worse off than they began.

Indulging in speculative history is a tricky business, but it is difficult to imagine that Lincoln, had he lived, would have permitted such an unhappy outcome. Although Johnson's Presidential Reconstruction followed Lincoln's Ten Percent Plan in most respects, Lincoln was never the racist that Johnson was, nor did he share Johnson's spitefulness and intransigence. In Wendell Phillips' 1863 Cooper Union speech, which generally criticized Lincoln, Phillips nevertheless praised the president as a "growing man." By this, he meant to acknowledge that Lincoln had grown to embrace emancipation and could, in the future, be expected to adopt other abolitionist views. In other words, Phillips recognized Lincoln's ability to identify meaningful political developments and shift his positions accordingly. Lincoln's sensitivity to public opinion, moreover, often kept him from pushing programs that might have been too extreme for the country at the time. In all likelihood, he would have behaved in much the same way in 1865 as Johnson did, but he would also have been capable of adapting to changes in the political situation as they occurred. Johnson was not.

Had Lincoln lived to see the Black Codes enacted, he undoubtedly would have heard the outcry of the freedpeople and responded in some way to their plight. Even more importantly, his response would have been carefully modulated to produce a morally and politically acceptable outcome, of which the Radicals simply weren't capable. Neither Stevens nor Sumner—and certainly not Andrew Johnson—shared Lincoln's incomparable ability to combine moral authority with such high-level political and rhetorical skills. These are the qualities that made Lincoln great, and their absence from Reconstruction destined the slaves he had freed to another hundred years of purgatory.

OPPOSITE: A large, almost festive crowd gathers in Paris, Texas, to watch the well-publicized 1893 lynching of Henry Smith, who had been accused of killing a young white girl.

PART THREE

FILMING LINCOLN

I've always been interested in telling a story of Abraham Lincoln. He's one of the most compelling figures in American history and in my life. I remember when I was taken at the age of four or five by my uncle to see the Lincoln Memorial. At first, I was terribly frightened by the immensity of the statue of Lincoln sitting in the chair. But as I got closer and closer, I was completely captivated by the comfort I found in looking at his face. Even though it was a white sculpture, there was a warmth and sense of safety I felt coming from him. I never forgot that moment.

—STEVEN SPIELBERG

STEVEN SPIELBERG (Director/Producer): "Lincoln guided our country through the worst crisis in its entire history. He helped the United States, and the idea of democracy as a viable political system, to survive. And more than any other single person, Lincoln helped end slavery. He didn't do this alone; many people contributed, from Frederick Douglass to all the abolitionists, to John Brown, and to the millions of slaves who resisted slavery. But it can be argued that the man who signed both the Emancipation Proclamation and the Thirteenth Amendment made the single greatest contribution to making slavery's end the grand consummation of the American Civil War."

RICK CARTER (Production Designer): "Having collaborated with Steven for more than quite a few years now, I would say that this movie represents an engagement not only with U.S. history, but also with the present, because it shows how a leader has to function in the face of great obstacles."

DORIS KEARNS GOODWIN (**Author of** *Team of Rivals*): "I knew there had been many books written about Lincoln, but I just thought that if I spent enough time researching, I could come up with a fresh angle. I wanted to bring him back to life. When I started, I thought I would write about Abe and Mary's relationship, but as I was reading about Lincoln's day-to-day activities, I began to see that he was spending more time with the members of his cabinet than he was with Mary. He took horseback rides with them in the afternoons and would go over to William Seward's house at night. It occurred to me that Lincoln was married to them even more than he was to Mary. When I realized they had all kept diaries and written hundreds of letters to their wives, I knew this was the story that I wanted to tell, especially because several of them had been Lincoln's rivals for the Republican nomination. It allowed me to show him through their eyes—intimate eyes—in a way that, hopefully, hadn't been done quite the same way before."

Tony Kushner (Screenwriter): "The very first time I had any contact with the Steven Spielberg universe was through Kathleen Kennedy, who called me after my play *Angels in America* was turned into a TV mini-series. We met and I asked what she and Steven were working on, and she replied, 'We're working on two films. One is about the murder of the Israeli Olympic athletes in Munich and the other is about Abraham Lincoln.' And that's where it started. I ended up writing *Munich*, after which Steven called me and said, 'Would you be willing to talk to me about working on the script for *Lincoln*?' I wanted to work with Steven again, but to me Lincoln seemed like an impossible subject.

"Later, Steven asked me to attend a conference he had organized with about fifteen of the country's leading experts on Lincoln. Afterward, Doris Kearns Goodwin pulled me aside and asked, 'What are you thinking?' I replied that I was terrified of doing this film and didn't think I should. And she said, 'I can't tell you if you'll succeed, but I can this: you'll never regret any time you spend with Abraham Lincoln.'"

Tony Kushner: "First, I decided I was going to start in the fall of 1863, when Salmon Chase challenged Lincoln for the Republican Party nomination in the upcoming 1864 presidential election. I thought if I started in the middle of 1863, I could get all the way to April 15, 1865, in about 150 pages. I started working and when I got to January 1864, I'd already written 140 pages. I tried three times, each time with the same result. I couldn't find a way to condense the material. Then the Writers' Guild went on strike, and that was actually a good thing for me creatively because I put the whole thing away for several months. When the strike was over, Steven and I decided to get together to discuss where we were with the film.

"The day before I was supposed to fly to Los Angeles, I realized that if we started the story in January 1865, with the fight for the Thirteenth Amendment, and then continued through till the end of Lincoln's life, there were incidents in those four months that were emblematic of the issues and dilemmas he faced during the four years of his administration. Steven really liked the idea.

"I started writing and by the time I was done, the script was 500 pages long. I sent it to Steven, with an apology, saying, 'I'm terribly sorry, this is insanely long, but I'm excited about a lot of it.' He started reading the script and, after reading the first fourth, which was about January 1865, he called me and said, 'It's exciting! I was wondering: is the amendment going to pass or not? Even though I knew that it would pass!'

"Over the course of the next three years of work, and especially once Daniel Day-Lewis came on board, the January amendment fight became the central focus of the script, until finally Steven said, when he'd finished reading the newest version of the January section, 'I think this is our film.'"

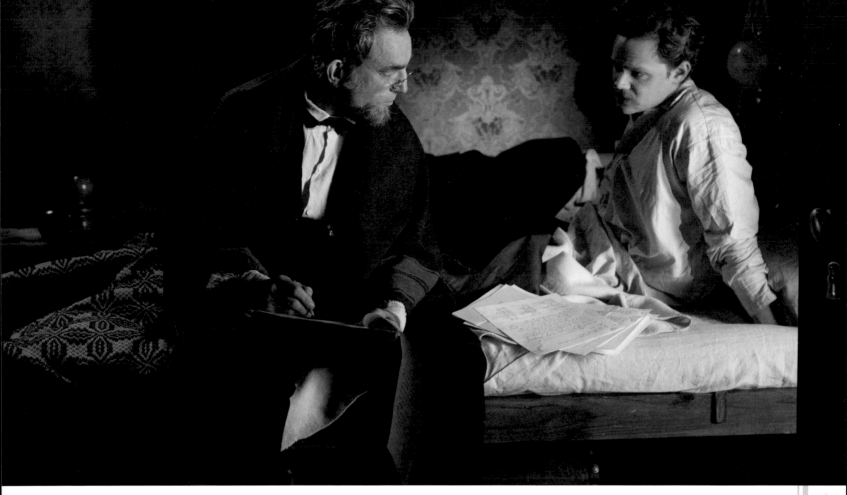

STEVEN SPIELBERG: "There are many feature-length stories to be found in Doris' eight-hundred-page *Team of Rivals*, but with Doris' blessing and her full participation throughout the process, we decided to focus on the ending of the war and the fight to abolish slavery through constitutional amendment. And we all feel that our film *Lincoln* is very true to the spirit of Doris' masterpiece."

DORIS KEARNS GOODWIN: "By choosing the last four months of the war, you not only get the beginning, middle, and end to the incredibly thrilling question of whether the Thirteenth Amendment is going to pass the Congress; you also get everything about Lincoln. You get his melancholy, his sense of humor, his deep conviction about the importance of passing this amendment. And you get his willingness to bear the weight of knowing that the price of passing this amendment may be the war going on even longer, because the South was willing to bargain if peace was on the table along with compromise on slavery. But he's saying, 'No, no compromise. On the contrary, I'm doubling down. And we're going to have this Thirteenth Amendment, not just the Emancipation Proclamation.'"

STEVEN SPIELBERG: "We focused on the last four months of Lincoln's life because we wanted to show Lincoln accomplishing something great, something really monumental—abolishing slavery and ending the Civil War. However, we also wanted to show that he was a man, not a monument. We thought our best hope of understanding and doing justice to this immensely complicated person was to depict him beginning, conducting, and then concluding a very complex action, which was the fight on the floor of the House of Representatives to pass the Thirteenth Amendment. And we wanted to include Lincoln's family dynamic, but only at the moments when it actually collided with the public events we were focusing on."

DORIS KEARNS GOODWIN: "In the winter of 2010, Steven asked if I would accompany Daniel Day-Lewis to Springfield, Illinois, and show him around the sites: Lincoln's house, the law offices, and the museum. As soon as we met, he put his arms around me and said, 'Oh, thank you so much for this book.' I immediately relaxed. We had the best time. The next day we went to Lincoln's house together, and you could sense that he was already feeling Lincoln."

STEVEN SPIELBERG: "I believe Daniel Day-Lewis and Tony Kushner understood Lincoln on a sub-atomic level—a level that goes well beyond anything I could articulate. I never asked Daniel about his process. I never questioned it. I just received the gift with tremendous gratitude. It was the same way with Tony. I never asked him how he was able to create those scenes and put those words together. I was standing next to two giant figures in the landscape of theater and art. I was in the middle constantly saying to myself, oh, don't mess this up, get these words, get that performance, get it in the best way you know how—but let them cast the giant shadows."

KATHLEEN KENNEDY (Producer): "Many people understand that with any role Daniel Day-Lewis plays, he goes through a total immersion. Lincoln was no exception. Prior to filming, he wanted to spend a great deal of time reading and understanding who Lincoln might have been. He spoke to Doris Kearns Goodwin quite a bit. He spent an enormous amount of time talking to Tony Kushner and to Steven, and went through his own process trying to find who Lincoln might have been as a man."

RICK CARTER: "Daniel came to the stage maybe five weeks before filming started. He was Daniel Day Lewis. He was seeing a set that was not even halfway constructed, but it was there in the bones. That was the last time I saw Daniel. When he arrived to start filming, he was President Lincoln."

KATHLEEN KENNEDY: "In many respects, Sally Field had one of the most difficult roles in the movie. A lot has been written about Mary Lincoln and how incredibly distraught and depressed she was, not only because of the loss of two children, but also because, at this point in the story, the war has been raging for years and there is so much sadness throughout the country. She experienced this sadness in her own family, and she watched the country go through it as well. Sally could have taken that and done something very predictable, but instead she found an incredible amount of restraint. So much of what Mary went through was overwhelming, but you understand the need for her to be the first lady and to support her husband."

SALLY FIELD (Mary Todd Lincoln): "I arrived in
Richmond a little more than a week before I was scheduled
to begin filming, but I knew Daniel was to start in just a few
days. I texted him, as Mary, trying to sound as if it pertained
to his presidency, and I said I knew the magnitude of the task
ahead of him but my only task was him. Therefore, I needed
to lay my eyes on him and perhaps even my hands. He kindly
invited me to his house for coffee the next morning. It was
important for me to be able to see and talk to him before we
were launched into space. After a while I said, 'In lieu of a carriage, get your shoes; we are going for a walk.' Which is what
we did. For two hours we walked and talked and laughed as
we strolled around the lovely Richmond neighborhood. When
we ended up back where we had started, I thanked him and
also warned him it was probably not the last time I would have
to be in his face. Daniel laughed. He is such a lovely, generous
man. A week later we were filming scenes, sometimes without
any rehearsal. Sometimes it just wasn't necessary."

STEVEN SPIELBERG: "So many of my
movies have had a visual outpouring of
imagery. I tell the story through pictures,
not words. In this case, the pictures took
second position to the language of Abraham
Lincoln—his actual language—that Tony
re-created based on his total immersion
in the way people spoke and wrote in this
nineteenth-century period. In that sense, I
took a backseat and watched this theatrical
experience evolve before my eyes."

KATHLEEN KENNEDY: "From early in the process, I remember discussing the incredible emotional impact of all the period photography that had been culled for research, reference, and inspiration. The images are stark and extremely visceral, haunting and beautiful at once. Much of our perception of the people, places, and daily life of the time is built from those photographic tableaus. And it is incredible how revealing these tableaus can be; just looking at pictures of Lincoln, you can feel the complexity of his character. The importance of finding those moments for the film, finding those single frames that could tell the story and convey where Lincoln was and what he was thinking, was very apparent. As you carry the memory of those images from one scene to the next, you find yourself immersed deeper and deeper into his world."

RICK CARTER: "For me as a production designer, the real opportunity and challenge of this movie was that while it is a big story, it's being told intimately. We're not standing back and showing you big vistas of things that Lincoln might not have seen; it's very much his world."

Steven Spielberg and Kathleen Kennedy

STEVEN SPIELBERG: "Many scenes play in one angle because I wanted the scenes to exist in seemingly real time. If I had gotten too fancy with too many reaction shots and too many cutaways, it would have drawn attention away from the very complicated political points that Lincoln was trying to make. I needed the audience to lean forward, to pay utter attention to what was being said by the characters. I didn't get fancy with the camera or in the cutting room, and John Williams' score is very soft and subtle, very much in the background."

JANUSZ KAMINSKI (Cinematographer): "There are various ways for a cinematographer to interpret a screenplay, but immediately it was very clear to me this was a story that should have a bit of restraint in terms of the photography. We should not make any specific color changes. We should not manipulate the negative. We should just photograph it in the most elegant way, simply because the language was so beautiful and the performances so stunning. Photography was merely there to record the actors' work and the screenwriter's words."

STEVEN SPIELBERG: "I wanted to step into the nineteenth century. I wanted to make a film that represented the times, the mood of the nation, and the mood of the individuals who were trying to solve problems. I wanted to feel a sense of authenticity on the set, where the only real imposition would be that there was a camera and there were monitors. I asked the actors, when they came onto the set, not to talk about the book they were reading, sports scores, or what was happening at home with their families, and to save all that for when they went outside the space we were shooting in. I didn't have to say it to everyone, actually. I made an announcement on the first day of shooting, and even those who had not heard it brought a reverential solidarity to their work and to their coworkers."

JOSEPH GORDON-LEVITT (Robert Lincoln): "Steven has a unique way of diving into the American zeitgeist and reflecting it in cinematic form. Obviously, the story of Abraham Lincoln is a prominent one in our culture, and I think he's the perfect guy to do it. He's clearly enjoying it. It's great to see a director having so much fun, because it doesn't always happen that way."

Janusz Kaminski: "All the actors were called by the names of the characters they played. Daniel was always the president. We felt that we were looking at the actual man, the actual president, not just because of the appearance, but because of the nobility of his behavior."

Sally Field: "I put myself in my own little shell and I stay in character as much as I can. It's how I work—how I've always worked—and it made total sense to me. It was a gift and a complete blessing, and I will always be grateful."

Kathleen Kennedy: "There was something seamless to what Daniel created and how he portrayed Lincoln. You weren't aware of the makeup. You were aware of the transformation, but he felt like a real person. He didn't feel like someone impersonating the president; he found who Lincoln was as a man—not just as the president, but as a father, a friend, and a husband. He found Lincoln's soul."

STEVEN SPIELBERG: "I was determined to make a movie about a working president, not a posing president. Abraham Lincoln was a statesman, a highly effective military leader. He was also a father, a husband, and everyone believes he was one of our country's greatest writers. He was intuitively brilliant; he always took the broad view, but he never lost his own ideals. He could almost see into the future, but he never forgot where he came from. All that he did was accomplished while looking deeply inside himself."

DAVID STRATHAIRN (William Seward): "[Steven] comes to the end of scenes where the human factor is the most important. You can have all this stuff dealing with the Thirteenth Amendment and then the scene will end on a moment between Lincoln and Tad, his youngest son—just a little human moment. To bring this huge issue down to this very human, palpable, and recognizable instance is, I think, part of what he does better than most."

KATHLEEN KENNEDY: "Steven has always had an incredible affinity for wonderful actors. He appreciates the art of acting. He would probably recognize it as one of the most important things he does as a director, and there's no question that the rapport he developed with Daniel Day-Lewis was second to none. I haven't seen him work with somebody that closely and that intimately in any other movie we've made together."

STEVEN SPIELBERG: "All the people who have played Lincoln in the past, from Henry Fonda to Raymond Massey, have portrayed him with a low, sepulchral voice, because people assume his voice should be senatorial, stentorian, and deep. That wasn't the case with Lincoln. It is widely reported that Lincoln had a surprisingly high voice, not a shrill one, but more of a tenor voice. That is why, when he spoke outdoors, his voice would carry over so many thousands of people, and why the 50,000 who gathered for the second inaugural address could hear every word he was saying."

DORIS KEARNS GOODWIN: "It was very important that Lincoln's sense of humor come across in the film. It was such an important part of my understanding of Lincoln that he could get himself out of his melancholy by telling these funny stories. He had hundreds of them."

JEREMY STRONG (John Nicolay): "I remember reading Lincoln say that, in regard to his humor, 'If it were not for this valve, I should die.'"

JANUSZ KAMINSKI: "The House of Representatives was the most challenging location simply because of the logistics. We went in order of the scenes and how the story unveils. If we had to cut back and forth between characters, we had to relight them in the same way as in previous shots. It's very hard to maintain lighting continuity when you're going from one character to another, and then back to the first character two days later."

GARY RYDSTROM (Sound Mixing): "The scenes in the House of Representatives were probably the most difficult to mix. But I took some pleasure in mixing them because all sound guys want fighting scenes, and the only fighting we really got was in the House. Eventually, the combination of good dialogue editing by John Knoll and the work of Andy Nelson, who mixed the dialogue, came out great. And I never heard Steven comment on dialogue this way before; it was a movie about words, and after the mix, the words were clear, and you could sense the performances as they had first been recorded on set by Ron Judkins."

KATHLEEN KENNEDY: "Tony's script and the power of his words are what draw you into this movie; it's what's being said and how it's being said that is so impactful. Steven wanted to capture the volatility of what went on in the House of Representatives and how all the issues were deeply argued and fought over in front of the people."

LEE PACE (Fernando Wood): "My character speaks in a way that you would never imagine people speaking in Congress today. They are so polite now. But these guys would just personally attack each other. I found that incredible, and I would ask Tony Kushner, is that real?"

S TEVEN SPIELBERG: "The slaves who were chained on the rafts
that Lincoln refers to when he's talking to Congressman Yeaman
was one of the few direct encounters Lincoln ever had with actual
slavery. For the most part, the men who in January 1865 passed the
Thirteenth Amendment had very little direct experience with the horrors of slavery. They had read newspaper accounts; they'd heard testi-
mony of escaped slaves. But few had ventured south to witness slaves
toiling in the fields. And the Northern constituents, we feel, were even
less likely to have direct experience with slavery. Those who hated slavery hated what they'd read of it. Even more important, I think, they
hated the idea of it. It was very important that the claustrophobia and
isolation of mid-nineteenth-century Washington be an essential part of
the telling of this story."

S. EPATHA MERKERSON (Lydia Smith): "After the amendment has been proposed and adopted, Thaddeus Stevens comes home with the copy to show Lydia. There's a moment where he asks her to read it for him and you see what it means to them both. She wasn't able to be there in the House with him because she is his housekeeper, but the first person that he thinks to bring it to is her. It's this lovely moment of triumph, love, and hope for the future. The one thing Steven kept saying was, it's the *awe* of the moment. Here is a black woman who has lived in the time her people were not free, when they not only didn't have rights, but were physically beaten, murdered. Women were raped and children were snatched from families. She had to have seen what this was. For her this moment must have been one of overwhelming release—and *awe*. It was the perfect word to use."

RICK CARTER: "Once the amendment has passed, we're in the last part of Lincoln's life, which I don't think many people know about. He didn't stay in Washington; he went down through Petersburg to Richmond, saw the battlefields, and negotiated with the peace commissioners from the South. What's interesting is to see his momentum toward the future, and then you realize he's going to the theater.

"At that point in the story, you imagine that there are only three options: you're either going to cut to the play, *Our American Cousin*, being performed; or you're going to cut to the president and his wife watching the play; or you're going to see John Wilkes Booth coming to assassinate the president. But that's not what happens. It's *Arabian Nights*. You see Tad, the youngest son. Suddenly, the curtains come down. A man comes out to address the audience and says, 'the president's been shot.' And this person you've spent the entire movie with is taken from you, but not in the way that you had expected."

SALLY FIELD: "*Lincoln* feels very current, on a world level, not just for the United States. What resonates so enormously is the difficulty, the messiness, the complicated nature of democracy, and how long it takes to have it really work. You have to want this noble notion of people governing themselves. You have to want it more than life."

HAL HOLBROOK (Francis Preston Blair, Sr.): "[Steven] concentrated on a political and moral conflict—a tremendous conflict that did not always go hand in hand—and has shown us how terribly difficult it is to achieve a moral victory in the middle of a political arena. And we can translate that in our own mind to the life of our country today, as we see it going by every twenty-four hours."

TONY KUSHNER: "The film has this very modest feeling that seems to me in keeping with the essential modesty of the man the movie is about. There's something Lincolnian about it—it's not melodramatic, it's not an enormous spectacle, it's not a great display of studio wealth. In a certain way, it's a small movie, but I think it digs into some very big issues, and it does that by focusing inward and staying within the realities that these people were trapped in. What you see is what was there."

STEVEN SPIELBERG: "I was lost when we finished the film. I know that Daniel was lost as well. I realized that I was no longer going to be on set in my tie, and share in working with one of the greatest actors, if not the greatest, I've ever collaborated with in my entire career. After the last shot, Daniel asked me to come into his trailer. He sat down and suddenly started talking to me in his English accent, as Daniel. Then tears came down my face, and it was very hard. It was a very tough pill to swallow because I think he let me down in the only way he could, and knew how to do, and he let himself down the same way. He instantly became himself.

"Of course, I think he was himself, with his wife and family, but I only got to see the Abraham Lincoln side of him. In that sense, I felt I got to know the president of the United States, arguably the greatest president of all. It wasn't a game we were playing; it wasn't method acting. When Daniel came onto the set, he was Abraham Lincoln, not just to me but also to the other actors in the scene and to the entire crew. It was a gift that he gave all of us, and it was a gift Tony Kushner gave to him to give to all of us. We all went home feeling a little emptier because we were not going to have that proximity any longer."

Tony Kushner (second from left) on set with Steven Spielberg (far right).

Tony Kushner: "Every era since Lincoln lived has appropriated him for various political purposes. The main relevance of Lincoln for now, and for all time, is that he proved it was possible to achieve progress, to achieve radical, even revolutionary transformation of society through electoral democracy. You turn to him over and over again because he is the ideal president, an ideal leader. He both led and followed the people, and made us realize what's great inside of us."

Kathleen Kennedy: "Lincoln exemplifies leadership. When you read his speeches and look back at how he conducted himself as president, it makes you realize how difficult it is for someone to live up to Lincoln's accomplishments in our day and age. This man, who was elected to hold fast the status quo, was able to bring together the most diametrically opposed individuals under the banner of union and progress. He got his hands dirty, he compromised when he could and dug in when he could not, and he bore the burden that came with keeping his countrymen mired in civil war as he paved the way for a brighter future. He did not do what was popular, but he did what was right.

"Throughout his presidency, Lincoln surrounded himself with many that shared few of his own opinions. Steven and Tony recognized that they needed to give very distinct voices to the dissent, to the counterarguments, and to the complexity of the politics. Steven recognized right from the beginning that he needed fantastic actors to immerse themselves in these roles, and with Tony's wonderful screenplay they created the tumult from which Lincoln had to find his own voice and choose a path for our country."

STEVEN **S**PIELBERG: "I've always believed that trying to make sense of what actually happened in the past helps to shape our present, and that history is always relevant in the sense that understanding how we got to where we are will help figure out where we want to go from here. Lincoln, specifically, is relevant today, to the present, because his presidency, I believe, offers the most vivid model of a leader and of leadership. Lincoln advocated things we still hold dear. He advocated that government could be a positive force for the good of all people. He advocated that democracy requires fairness and compassion and education. And it requires a respect for law as well as racial, ethnic, and religious tolerance—and sometimes a good sense of humor."

PART FOUR

Bringing History to Life

For me it always starts with trying to find something on the inside so that I can work from the inside out. The heart of this movie is Lincoln's office, where he did most of his work as president. I always felt it was important to have it be as close as possible to the real office as we know it. That level of detail, whether it be a battle map, a little note, or pictures on the wall, wasn't about being painstaking. It was more about doing a service to the actors and the storytellers. From that point on, we were as accurate as we could be.

—Rick Carter

Past Lives

"ITAKE a great deal of responsibility for all the characters that I portray," Gloria Reuben says. "But when the character is someone who actually lived, I want that portrayal to be as true to life as possible.

"This is only the second time that I've played a person who actually walked the earth," Reuben continues. "The first time, I portrayed Condoleezza Rice in David Hare's play *Stuff Happens.* For that role, I watched footage of her, listened to how she spoke, observed the way she interacted with other people; and that gave me a sense of who she was and what might be lying beneath the surface. Unfortunately, I couldn't do that with Elizabeth Keckley."

Unlike many of the other characters in *Lincoln,* seamstress Elizabeth Keckley didn't lead a well-documented life. The only surviving primary sources are a book (Keckley's 1868 autobiography) and two photographs, one taken during Keckley's time with the Lincolns and another taken many years later. Reuben consulted numerous secondary sources as well, including books describing Keckley's close relationship with Mary Lincoln, but none proved so meaningful to her as the photograph of Keckley in her early forties. "Reading those books was helpful, but there was something about that photograph of the younger Elizabeth—the look on her face—that drew me in. Her gaze was so direct and so deep, there was such a strength and dignity in her stance, that I felt immediately connected to her."

Wanting to deepen that connection, Reuben decided to visit the landscape of Keckley's childhood in Virginia and North Carolina. Shortly before shooting began, she

This carte-de-visite photograph of Elizabeth Keckley inspired Gloria Reuben (opposite) to connect with her character.

moved to Richmond and set up a base of operations from which she made day trips to places described in Keckley's memoirs. "Many of those places have become historic sites, so it was easy for me to remain incognito," Reuben says. "But when I visited Hampden-Sydney College, where Elizabeth had lived as a young girl and where she was first beaten, the campus was so busy with students moving in that it was hard for me to get around. Finally, I threw caution to the wind and went to the office and told them what I was doing. They guided me to the part of the campus where they believed the slave quarters had been, and I walked all over that ground.

"There's nothing like being in the physical environment where a person lived," Reuben explains. "It goes so much deeper than reading about it in a book."

All of Reuben's research came together for her on the day that costume designer Joanna Johnston dressed her for the first time in the garment she would wear. "I remember that day particularly well," Reuben says. "We put on the dress, which was very similar to the one in the photograph of Elizabeth, and we did up all the buttons. I already had my makeup on, and my hair was pulled back and parted like Elizabeth's. So when I glanced in the mirror, my breath caught in my throat. The effect was unbelievable. I felt I had really tapped into her."

As little information as Reuben had about Elizabeth Keckley, James Spader had even less about William N. Bilbo. The Nashville lawyer didn't write memoirs, and no image of him survives. All Spader had to work with were the letters Bilbo wrote to Secretary of State William

Seward during the winter of 1864–65, reporting on his lobbying efforts, and the occasional mentions of Bilbo in the diaries and letters of contemporaries.

"First and foremost, I'm devoted to the script," Spader says. "No matter what the project is, that's the prism through which I interpret everything. I don't create the characters I play; the screenwriters and film-makers do that. But when I'm working with historical subjects, I do have to respect the facts and try to temper my ignorance."

Lacking much specific character history, Spader immersed himself in what he calls "context"—that is, the accumulation of detail that gives each historical era its unique human character. "One of the things I find enor-mously helpful is imagery, because from imagery comes context," he says. "Even when a character is involved in weighty historical events, he still has to get up in the morning, get dressed, and go to the bathroom. He still has to eat a meal, brush his hair, and walk down the street. These are the things that make it possible for me to play the character."

To get a sense of Bilbo's context, Spader watched and rewatched all eleven hours of Ken Burns' *The Civil War* documentary. "I saw people's faces," he says. "I saw where they lived and how they lived. I saw the streets they walked on and how they dressed and how they tied their ties. I could even tell how often they might have bathed.

"Also, that documentary is chock-full of firsthand accounts, which I love because they tell me what people were talking about and reading at the time," Spader con-tinues. "Compared to facts and figures, they're much more subjective—which works for me, because my job is incredibly subjective. I have to depict historical events, but I also have to serve the drama. That's why I had to walk a fine line with this character. If I delved too deeply into the nature of Bilbo, I might learn something that could subvert what I needed to do to serve the drama."

The three political operatives in *Lincoln* are unusual characters because, in addition to fulfilling their own his-torical roles, screenwriter Tony Kushner and director Steven Spielberg used them as composites to represent the actions of several other lobbyists who couldn't be included in the film. Adding more cast to a film that already had 140 speaking roles "would simply have been gratuitous," Spader explains. "So Steven and Tony distilled all of the lobbyists into three characters—Bilbo, Latham, and

A November 22, 1864, letter from William N. Bilbo, portrayed by James Spader (opposite), "recently from the South," to President Lincoln, requesting an interview to communicate "important information."

Schell. This deviates a little from what actually happened, but it's a way of presenting the landscape and activities of the lobbyists while still serving the drama."

The character of Bilbo, in particular, served the drama by providing some irreverence and comic relief. "The events depicted in this film were so burdensome and the decisions so grave that we needed a counter-point," Spader says. "That was clear to me from the first time I read the screenplay, and Steven and I talked about it from the very beginning. Once I arrived on the set, Daniel [Day-Lewis] and I also talked about it. They were both counting on me to bring a hint of irreverence to the story, which was otherwise so reverential. The weight of the world was resting on Lincoln's shoulders at that time, and there needed to be some balance in the storytelling. The Bilbo character was an important part of creating that balance.

"Whether you're playing a historical figure or not, you come to the set with a character in mind—a sense of how he will respond to a given set of circumstances—and then you see what happens," Spader continues. "You need to allow for a certain amount of latitude, because you're a human being and you're playing across from other human beings, who will surprise you. You can have an idea in your head going in, but if you're really success-ful, something else will usually happen. That's why I do all of my homework in advance; and when I get to the set, I put it all away. I don't want to crowd my mind with facts and figures, because that just limits the spontaneity."

Sally Field, who plays Mary Todd Lincoln, agrees. "You have to gather as much information as you can so that you can find a human link between yourself and the character," she says. "Then you have to let the information go, but not the link that makes the character yours.

"The task of an actor," she continues, "is to learn as much as you can about a character so that you can put yourself into that person's shoes. Does she have a tendency to react this way or that, to feel this way or that, because of something that happened to her long ago? You need to figure that out, and you need to let it go. Then you walk out onto the set and whatever happens, happens. But you have to keep with you that emotional link to how the person would have behaved."

Director Steven Spielberg shares a few thoughts with Sally Field.

In researching Mrs. Lincoln, Field paid particular attention to the subtleties of her daily life in Illinois. "I was very interested in what she did during her downtime, while she waited for her husband to come home each day," Field recalls. "Did she do needlepoint? Crewel work? Did she only read? I was desperate to find out, and I learned that she did all the family's sewing, even though she hated it. She was a lady, and ladies had to have embroidered linens, but there wasn't anyone else to do it. She couldn't afford to pay, so she did the needlework herself."

Beyond the research, Field prepared for the role physically by adjusting her weight. "I'd worked with Sally before, on *Forrest Gump*," Joanna Johnston says, "and we decided the first time we spoke about *Lincoln* that she should put on a substantial amount of weight. She and Mary Todd are both the same height, which was good. But Sally's very slim, while Mary Todd had this brilliant sort of plump physicality."

"We decided that I should make my measurements the same as Mary Todd's so that when I was corseted into the dress, I would look the way she did," Field concurs. "And I did it. I gained twenty pounds. But Joanna kept saying to me, 'Why can't you make some of it go to your arms?' And I said, 'Joanna, there's nothing I can do. It just goes to my butt and stays there!'"

According to Field, once she finishes her preparation and takes on the guise of a character, the film becomes her new reality. "You sort of hypnotize yourself, and the set becomes your cocoon," she says. "'This is the reality,' you tell yourself. 'This is who you are. This is where you live. This is your life.' And you have all this fabulous talent around to help you perpetuate the illusion. When you're in the clothes and the hair and the rest, you really feel you're in that era, and your emotionality can come out."

The actors' emotionality came out memorably on the last day of shooting, when the cast performed *Lincoln*'s final scene. "I don't think any of us will forget that," Field says. "Mary kisses her husband's hand good-bye, and she's ushered out of the room while he lies there, dying. By that time, I don't think any of us knew the difference between film and reality, including Steven. The work had taken on a life of its own.

"Experiences are funny things to actors," Field continues. "We work so hard to make the characters real to us that what happens to them seems real to us, too. Because we create these characters out of real things from our own lives, our own feelings, we link to them in such a way that our brains, which don't know the difference, record the scenes we play as though they were real experiences. So when we remember, our brains put out the same brain waves and our glands put out the same hormones as if the memories were of actual life experiences. That's what you work for and what you ride like a wave. It feels like the *Titanic* is going down, and you're on it."

OPPOSITE: **Mary Lincoln (Sally Field) agonizes over her son's decision to enlist in the Union army.**

Looking Back

ALMOST everyone who worked on *Lincoln* began his or her research with the photographs. The first president to be photographed was William Henry Harrison, who posed inside the Capitol before stepping out into the rain on his inauguration day. The art of photography was only two years old then, having been invented in 1839 in France by Louis Daguerre; but it had already spread to New York City, where Mathew Brady became one of its earliest American practitioners. Brady opened his own studio in 1844 and a year later began exhibiting portraits of famous Americans there. In 1849, he opened a second studio in Washington; and by 1860, he had become the country's premier photographic portraitist, politicians his specialty. The thousands of images he and his employees recorded during the early and mid-1860s proved to be an invaluable resource for the filmmakers.

"The great thing was that we were just in time," costume designer Joanna Johnston explains. "The 1860s were the first era in which photography was immensely popular, so there's a brilliant amount of documentation. Only a few people didn't have their pictures taken."

"A lot has been written about that period in American history," production designer Rick Carter says, "but I

OPPOSITE: A tintype of Abraham Lincoln, the first American politician to grasp fully the political usefulness of the new medium of photography.

Photographer Mathew Brady

started with the photographs, especially the ones of Lincoln. He's the first president to have been photographed extensively before he entered office and then while he was in office. You can really see his progression through his term, from the beginning of the war to the end. Then there are all those images of the war. Because of them, we remember the Civil War in a fundamentally different way than we do the Revolutionary War or the War of 1812, which seem much less real to us."

The filmmakers also relied on textual sources, of course, both primary and secondary. In order to gain insight into his character's personality, James Spader read a series of letters that William N. Bilbo (whom Spader plays) wrote to Secretary of State William Seward, reporting on his lobbying efforts. Similarly, Jeremy Strong, who plays Lincoln secretary John Nicolay, spent several days in the Library of Congress Reading Room examining letters that Nicolay had written to his fiancée. Also while at the Library of Congress, Strong learned from a reference in an 1880s journal (discovered by Civil War and Reconstruction Specialist Michelle Krowl) that Nicolay, although born in Bavaria, had no discernible German accent. Apparently, after arriving in the United States at the age of six, Nicolay had learned to speak English like a native, so Strong portrayed him that way.

The most important secondary source for *Lincoln* was *Team of Rivals: The Political Genius of Abraham*

This handkerchief belonged to Mary Todd Lincoln, who presumably embroidered the "ML" monogram because she did most of her own needlework.

Lincoln by Doris Kearns Goodwin. "In *Team of Rivals*, Doris paints a very distinct portrait of Lincoln that really inspired Tony [Kushner] and Steven [Spielberg]," producer Kathleen Kennedy reports. "Because so much has been written about Lincoln, it can be difficult to figure out who he was and what he was like, how he thought and what made him tick, among all the conflicting opinions. Doris' great contribution was to give us a clear interpretation."

"The book that I found most helpful was Catherine Clinton's biography of Mary Lincoln," recalls Sally Field, who plays Mrs. Lincoln in the film. "Catherine actually came down at one point to have dinner with me; and I told her how important her book was to me. Instead of giving her own opinions as to what was going on with Mary, she simply stated the facts, said what everyone else thought they meant, and then let me draw my own conclusions."

Field found especially helpful the information in Clinton's book on Mary's married life. "Most of my scenes were with Daniel [Day-Lewis]," Field explains. "When you're playing someone with a long married life, there has to be a connection, an intimacy, that you can't fake. You have to find that place where human beings know each other so well, and their physicality together becomes incredibly important. You really have to know where they are sexually. Do they touch each other, or is there just an unconscious intimacy between them? All of that

plays even if you never speak about it, even if the scenes are about something else. Catherine's book was especially good for me because it gave me that sort of information."

When the filmmakers weren't reading or looking at photographs, they also took field trips. Gloria Reuben, for instance, visited the childhood homes of her character, Elizabeth Keckley, while Jeremy Strong visited Civil War battlefields. Somewhat more unusual was a visit that Field and Johnston made to the Los Angeles home of Louise Taper, a prominent collector of Lincoln artifacts. "She has all sorts of small possessions that belonged to Mary Todd, like nightdresses and handkerchiefs and prayer books," Johnston remembers. "But I was particularly taken with the hand casts of President Lincoln. I hadn't realized how large they were. Huge, really huge. When I saw the casting—that was really quite something. It really moved me."

Field even consulted an audio source. To get Mrs. Lincoln's accent just right, the actor borrowed from a dialect coach tapes of elderly women from the area around Lexington, Kentucky, where Mary Todd had been born and raised. "The tapes were recorded in the 1980s, when the women speaking were in their eighties, so they weren't that far removed from the Civil War era," Field explains. "Even though their accents had become a little homogenized, you could still hear a little of the way people used to speak in that part of the country."

"When you make a movie like this, it's important to utilize as many resources as possible," Kennedy says. "We went to the Library of Congress, we had conversations with Doris, we had conversations with other historians—we tried to breathe life into the story any way we could, whether that meant looking at photographs or going to museums or visiting historic sites. Usually, you're looking for visual material. You may not use what you find literally, but you hope it will inform the overall look so that the film feels authentic, from the sets and the costumes and the makeup to the photography and the lighting and the way the gaslight makes the room fall off into darkness. Things like that dictate your approach to the color and texture of fabrics, for example, and they become part of the authenticity of the time."

OPPOSITE: For a scene with Mary and Abraham Lincoln, director Steven Spielberg offers some guidance (top).

Clothed in History

WHILE most feature films employ perhaps forty actors with speaking roles, *Lincoln* had 140, all of whom had to be clothed in historically accurate period dress. "It felt completely unlike any other film I've done," costume designer Joanna Johnston says. "It seemed like such a marathon going through, but I'm proud to have completed it and just rather amazed at what we collectively achieved."

The enormous size of the cast forced Johnston to devise a complex management strategy. "In filmmaking, you're always restricted by time and money, so there is inevitably a certain amount of compromise," she says. "It really becomes a question of what shortcuts can you take without losing the integrity of what you're doing."

Johnston's strategy with *Lincoln* was to divide the cast into two groups of about seventy actors each. For one group, the principal characters, she custom-made all of the actors' clothing; for the other group, the secondary characters, she manufactured a pool of stock clothing that could be adapted as necessary to meet the needs of a particular scene. "With the scenes set in the House of Representatives, for example, we had a lot of actors who were practically day players," Johnston explains. "We used the stock clothing for them; and then as the filming went on, we recycled things, using the same garments in different ways."

Johnston also realized at the start that the wardrobes of the principal characters—with the notable exception of Mary Todd Lincoln—couldn't be as extensive as she would have liked. "Early on, I had a conversation with Steven [Spielberg]," Johnston recalls, "and I suggested to him using just a single look for most of the male characters, including Lincoln. He liked the idea, and Daniel

ABOVE: **Illustration of Daniel Day-Lewis as Lincoln in a costume created by Joanna Johnston.**

[Day-Lewis] was keen on it, too. You establish the man, and then you hold the man.

"There were exceptions, of course," she continues. "A few of the leading males had variances that were appropriate to their characters—such as Seward, who dressed carefully. Others got small shifts, often different vests, that helped with the depiction of the days changing. But the majority had just the one set of clothing."

With this costuming strategy in mind, the British-born Johnston began researching American clothing styles of the mid-nineteenth century. Fortunately, by the 1860s, the relatively new medium of photography had become extremely popular in the United States, providing Johnston with a wide range of period images, including multiple portraits of nearly all the major characters. "I got most of my information from those photographs," Johnston says. "Even though the portraits were formal and rather stiff, I could still tell what type of people they were. Even from the chest up, it's possible to see whether someone's sloppy or mannered or conscientious in the way he presents himself. I also took from the photographs information about the cloth each man was wearing—whether it was heavy or light or had a sheen—and used that information to create a look for each of the cast."

The photography had its limits, however. Because it was all monochrome, Johnston had to look elsewhere for information about fabric color. Fortunately, as an expert on antique clothing, she was already familiar with the mid-nineteenth century color palette for men, which was nearly uniformly black. The potential for monotony concerned her, however, especially because the cast had so many males. So she decided to give the frock coats, in particular, an "arc and curve" of color in order to help audiences distinguish one character from another. "With

so many men in the cast, we had to be careful not to make them all look the same," Johnston says. "So instead of dressing all of the male characters in solid black, we used a variety of off-blacks—including dark forest greens, dark browns, and aubergines—which we peppered into the solid blacks to break things up. Your mind thinks they're all solid blacks, but in reality there has been a shift, and we worked hard to get that shift in there."

The women's clothing required more diverse research. In addition to the photographic sources she had already accumulated, Johnston surveyed contemporary paintings and consulted Parisian fashion plates of the early 1860s. American periodicals routinely obtained these illustrations, which showed what was fashionable in Europe at the time, and adapted them for the domestic market. They're what Mary Todd Lincoln would have looked at and given to seamstresses like Elizabeth Keckley. "As a European, I really enjoy looking at the American interpretation of women's clothing," Johnston says. "Especially in their pattern and scale, the American fashions were so much stronger, bolder, and altogether more dramatic."

Given Johnston's strong interest in women's clothing, it shouldn't be surprising that she spent a disproportionate amount of her time clothing the three primary female characters, especially Mary Todd Lincoln. "At the start of this project, I knew nothing about Mary Todd, except that she was an odd-looking creature who spent a lot of money on clothes and seemed to annoy everyone," Johnston recalls. "But as I learned more about her, I became incredibly fascinated by her character. She seems to be a very misrepresented person and was probably rather extraordinary. When you begin to study her, you learn that she was incredibly conscientious about the way she dressed, and she had a very particular style. That's why such a great volume of work

Illustration of Joanna Johnston's uniform design for Robert Lincoln (Joseph Gordon-Levitt).

ABOVE: Joanna Johnston's design of a dress for Mary Todd Lincoln (Sally Field).

OPPOSITE: Sally Field in the "wrapper" dress.

went into Mary Todd—because she had such a huge closet in her life, and we needed to give that sense of her."

Most of the clothing that Johnston created for Sally Field fits within the style of Mrs. Lincoln's actual wardrobe. But one garment matches a historical dress exactly—the "wrapper" dress, now in the collection of the Chicago History Museum. Using measurements and photographs provided by the curators, Johnston was able to re-create the dress down to the stitching. "Reproducing the wrapper dress was an incredibly vital exercise for me," Johnston says. "Most of the other clothing we were doing for Mary Todd was 'in the essence of' and not exactly what she wore. But re-creating the wrapper dress informed everything else we made for Sally."

Clothing Mary Todd's husband was an altogether different matter. Unlike his wife, Abraham Lincoln wasn't much interested in clothes. "For the president, clothing was purely a way of keeping out the weather," Johnston says. "He didn't really wear clothes; they just hung on him. Mary Todd tried to smarten him up,

but he wouldn't have it because he wanted to stay a man of the people. So his coats had frayed cuffs, his shirts had stains on them, and he remained a rather shambolic-looking creature."

In keeping with her one-look approach, Johnston searched for an appropriate suit from the last years of the president's life. She found one at the Smithsonian Institution. "I couldn't get there," she explains. "But Michael Sloan, my tailor, and Dave Crossman, the costume supervisor, visited the museum and got permission to inspect the suit closely. They took a mass of photographs and measurements, and we all worked together from those.

"The silhouette of the look was the key—the hang of the coat, the feel of his body within, the gentleness of the cloth and color," Johnston continues. "The coat in the Smithsonian was probably close to black when it was made, but over the years the cloth had turned slightly warmer, which often happens to fabric as it ages. My instinct was to carry this warmth into the reproduction, too. We tested various options and eventually got to this beautiful dark walnut that the camera shows as a soft, warm hue wrapping around the president's body. I think it really punctuates the man."

Groomed for Posterity

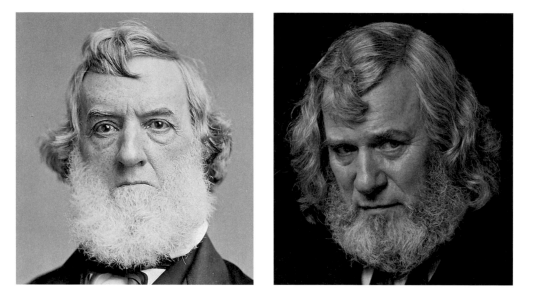

Secretary of the Navy Gideon Welles (left) and Grainger Hines

"MOST people understand that when you're making a period film, you have to pay a lot of attention to the way the actors are dressed and the way the sets are decorated. However, very few people think about the hair," observes Lois Burwell, who developed the hair and makeup for *Lincoln* (along with hair department head Kay Georgiou). "The way an actor's hair looks can make all the difference in whether an audience finds the character believable."

Burwell begins every historical project with research. In this case, she studied photographs from the 1850s and 1860s to see how Americans of the period looked. "People—men especially—don't look the way they did in 1865," she explains. "It's not just facial hair and hair length; it's subtleties like shape and texture. Men wore hats then, so when they came indoors and took them off, their hair had a hat shape. Also their hair wasn't squeaky clean and conditioned the way men's hair is today. Yes, they washed their hair, but not as often and not with the same products. If you look at those old photographs, you'll see the hat shape, and you'll see the oily sheen.

Those are the subtleties that let you know it's 1865."

In addition to the miscellaneous portraits she examined, Burwell also studied images of the principal characters whose likenesses have survived. "You look for all the photographs you can find within a ten-year period, more or less," Burwell says. "Obviously, portraits of people when they were eight years old won't be very helpful, but people do tend to follow through on things, normally sticking with the look of their heyday, so almost any adult photograph will give you a sense of the person and how that person looked, even if you can't find a picture from 1865."

Once the actors were cast, Burwell and Georgiou met with each of them to assess what needed to be done to make the actor more closely resemble the historical character he or she was playing. In some cases, there was a complicating factor: both the actor's face and the historical character's face were very well known. "Take an iconic figure like Grant," Burwell says. "Everyone knows what he looks like, but Jared Harris came in clean-shaven with short 1960s back and sides because he was

ABOVE: Lt. Gen. Ulysses S. Grant (left) and Jared Harris TOP: Lois Burwell tends to Jared Harris' bristles.

in the middle of shooting *Mad Men*. The same for Joseph Gordon-Levitt, who came straight from *The Dark Knight Rises* with short back and sides."

There are prosthetics that Burwell could have used to increase these actors' resemblance to their characters, but such measures were never an option. "To be honest, we didn't have the time or budget to do them," she says. "So it became a makeup and hair challenge—without a doubt, a makeup and hair challenge."

Burwell brought on Terry Jarvis, her associate of thirty years, to make all the facial hair that would be needed, which was a lot. "Without Terry on location, we'd really have been stuffed," she recalls. "In a few cases, there was some late casting, or people would turn up clean-shaven, and you'd say to yourself, 'Oh, blimey!' It could have been a logistical nightmare. But having someone of Terry's tremendous skill and speed with us meant that we could rise to the occasion, which contributed enormously to the look of the film."

The most important beard in the film, however, was natural—or mostly natural. Daniel Day-Lewis grew his own beard for *Lincoln*; but it came in lighter than the president's, so it had to be dyed—not a single shade of black, because that would have looked fake, but multiple colors, here and there, a single strand at a time.

With the help of her second, Kenny Myers, Burwell also augmented Day-Lewis' features using a method called stretch and stipple. Every day, they painted a resin on Day-Lewis' face and shaped it as it dried—a precise and exacting process. "There's no way around it," Burwell says. "It isn't something you just pop out of a mold. You have to paint it on fresh. We used it on Daniel to give his face some age and change some of its character."

Although no other actor required this high degree of skin treatment, all of the male cast members—and there were a lot of them—needed to have their head hair and facial hair treated every day. "Even the actors who grew magnificent beards of their own needed work," Burwell says, "because men today are absolutely clueless about grooming their beards. After all, these weren't woodsmen's beards we were re-creating. They were fashionable beards of the nineteenth century. Every morning, we'd dress all the beards with pomades and pull them out to make them look right. I mean, we would literally get our hands in there, pull the beards out and curl them or put in clips, and then spray them to give them style and shape."

Not only the principal cast members but also the day players and extras got this treatment, which created a few logistical challenges. For the large House of Representatives scenes, which featured fifty-eight actors with speaking roles, Burwell and Georgiou had to hire twenty-five additional hairstylists and twenty-five additional makeup artists to handle the 225 extras. "Whenever these people came in for costume fittings, usually three or four days in advance, we'd also put them through hair and makeup," Burwell recounts. "We'd cut their hair and fit them with wigs or facial hair from our stock, if they needed it. Essentially, we'd do whatever we could to make them look acceptable in the nineteenth century. Then, on the day of the shoot, we'd work on them again, shaping and styling to get the right feel."

Even the extras required careful attention because of the "odd one out" principle. "If something doesn't look like it belongs, it's a distraction," Burwell explains. "The same thing applies to actors in period films. If a single actor doesn't look true to the period, then the scene won't work visually—but, strangely, it's the other actors, the ones who do fit the period, who seem odd, not the single modern one. The group doesn't compensate for the individual, because the curtain has been pulled back to reveal the artifice.

"I just pray that there's not a moment in the film when the audience thinks, 'Oh, there's an actor in makeup,'" Burwell continues. "If they don't notice it at all, if no one ever notices the hair and makeup, and they just think the actor bears an uncanny resemblance to a historical person, so that all they do is concentrate on the story, *then* I'll be pleased."

> **T**HERE are some things, like taking proper care of a beard, that have been lost. We like to think of ourselves as being at the height of cosmetics, and we look down at the nineteenth century. "Oh, they had such terrible teeth then and such filthy hair." But there are actually some things that human beings did far better in 1865, and caring for beards is one of them.
>
> **—LOIS BURWELL**

ABOVE: The Virginia State Capitol in Richmond with the false portico added by the production team.
OPPOSITE: The White House interior sets included the second-floor hallway (top) and Mary Lincoln's bedroom.

AMONG the production designer's many responsibilities are scouting a film's locations and constructing its sets. As one might imagine, the logistical and aesthetic considerations are daunting; but Rick Carter, who designed the production of *Lincoln*, had an even greater challenge: the locations he found and the sets he built had to be historically authentic as well as cost effective and aesthetically pleasing. In other words, he had to re-create Washington as it appeared in 1865, especially the second floor of the White House and the chamber of the House of Representatives.

"When you do what I do," Carter says, "you're trying to create a verisimilitude, an appearance of truth, that conveys the spirit of what you think is important about the film. There's a bag of tricks you use—aging objects, covering paved streets with dirt, all sorts of things—but it all comes down to being in the right place. We could have used a green screen and digitization, of course, but that's expensive—and, anyway, we weren't making that kind of film."

Although Carter spent several years visiting every possible location in the United States and Canada, his epiphany didn't come until late one night when he found himself standing outside the West Wing, waiting for a rainstorm to pass. He had just completed an after-hours tour of the White House, and everyone had gone home except his tour guide, who wanted to leave, too. It was raining hard,

Reconstruction of a Different Sort

however, so the guide suggested that Carter wait under an eave until the rain let up before showing himself out through the Pennsylvania Avenue gate.

"There I was, standing alone outside the West Wing, with the North Portico of the White House to my right, and I just felt this amazing sense of intimacy, knowing that Lincoln had often walked from that portico across the street to the War Department—that would have been his path," Carter remembers. "So I decided to step out into the rain, and I stood there for half an hour, looking back at the White House and imagining him walking over the same ground to get the latest news of the war."

While Carter stood in the rain, staring at the North Portico, a thought occurred to him. "It struck me," he says, "that by adding a portico to the north side of the Virginia State Capitol in Richmond, I could make the two buildings look very similar. I also felt there was an almost spiritual connection between the White House and the Virginia capitol, because of the capitol's ties to

the Civil War, and I wanted to work with that connection. So I recommended Richmond to Steven [Spielberg] and Kathleen [Kennedy]; they went along, and that's what we did."

With the cooperation of the state of Virginia, the filmmakers were able to take over Richmond's Capitol Square for several weeks of filming. They had to wait until the legislature was out of session, of course, but that provided an additional benefit. "We needed a place to double as the House of Representatives, and there aren't many legislative chambers that look right," Carter says. "A reproduction was built for *Transformers*, and we thought we could use that; but by the time we were ready to go, it had been demolished, and we couldn't afford to build one of our own. Luckily, the capitol—that is, the same building I wanted to use for the White House exteriors—also happened to have a legislative chamber that was perfect for the scenes in the House."

Although the chamber of the Virginia House

Filming in the chamber of the House of Delegates, Richmond.

of Delegates is only half the size of the actual House of Representatives chamber, Carter saw that it was well maintained, painted in an aesthetically pleasing way, and could be photographed effectively. But its greatest advantage, he says, was that "Steven and the actors could walk in and feel the sense of purpose that historic places like that have."

In other ways as well, Richmond turned out to be the perfect location. The historic buildings in Capitol Square and others in the Old Towne section of nearby Petersburg looked

A Richmond street altered by the production team to give it the appearance of Washington, D.C., in 1865.

more like 1865 Washington than even Washington does today. Carter is still grateful to those in the state and local governments who allowed him the location control he needed to make the shoots happen. "It was like filming on a back lot," he says. "We were able to control access totally, so there were no gawkers and nothing to distract the actors."

The capitol groundskeepers even agreed to stop mowing the lawns three months in advance of the shoot. "You know, it was wartime," Carter explains, "and I just didn't think they would have gone to the same trouble grooming the White House lawn as if there hadn't been a war on."

For the White House interiors, Carter found an empty warehouse in Richmond and built a conventional set, which Jim Erickson decorated. "By the time I come along," Erickson says, "the physical spaces are already decided, and it's my job to fill them in. I have to find furniture, art, carpets, light fixtures—everything."

Like nearly everyone else who worked on the production of *Lincoln*, Erickson began by studying contemporary photographs and drawings of the Lincoln White House. Particularly helpful was a sketch of Lincoln's office drawn by C. K. Stellwagen in late 1864, which showed the type and arrangement of the furniture. Other items on Erickson's to-find list were dictated by the script. "If there was a scene in which the president read a book," Erickson says, "then I needed to get him

a lamp to read it by." Erickson also needed to reproduce documents for Lincoln's office, so he contacted the White House Historical Association to ask what Lincoln's stationery looked like. Then he printed some up.

When Lincoln was president, the White House didn't have a West Wing, and all of the first-floor rooms were used for public functions; so the president's office was on the second floor, just down the hall from his living quarters (a hall that was often uncomfortably crowded with petitioners). The set that Carter built reproduced the entire second floor, but the president's office was its core.

"We tried to re-create that office with as much accuracy as we possibly could, and I'd like to think that we did about as good a job as anyone has or ever will," Carter says. "There are certainly things we don't know, but the amount of research we did allowed us to re-create the office in a way that's really close to what it would have been like."

To find objects for the set, Erickson and his crew frequented local antique shops, flea markets, and auctions. "I always look for good local auctions," Erickson says. "I checked online and didn't see anything too interesting, but someone told me about a place called Alexander's that had auctions every Thursday night. So I went, and, my

ABOVE: C. K. Stellwagen's October 1864 sketch of Lincoln's office. The annotations record details of the room, including color information.

BELOW: The president's cabinet met regularly on Tuesdays and Fridays in the president's office.

God, it was like, a showroom filled with everything I needed. There were pieces of High Victorian furniture everywhere; and because that style is out of fashion, they were going dirt cheap." Erickson happened to be searching at the time for a bed to put in Mary Lincoln's bedroom. He'd found a suitable frame at a store in Oklahoma, but it was very pricey—eighteen thousand dollars. At Alexander's, he found an equally good option for just eighteen hundred dollars. "Things like that would just turn up," he says.

Meanwhile, Erickson had to make choices about what to buy and what to reproduce. That is, which objects could be "close enough," and which had to be exact? "You can't research every single nailhead," he says. "What you've got to do is get your head into the mode of the project and let your intuition kick in. Your brain becomes open to the period, and then you know what to do."

Carter & Company used the photograph of Lincoln in his office (above) to re-create the office's wallpaper (right).

For example, for the desk in Lincoln's office, Erickson decided against a reproduction. Instead, he bought an original plantation desk similar in size and style and then altered it to make it an even closer match. "There's an honesty and an integrity to period furniture that you don't get with reproductions," Erickson says. "On the other hand, I had to build the table in Lincoln's office from scratch because it was very odd and specific, and I just couldn't find anything like it."

The pièce de résistance in the office, however, was the wallpaper. Normally, Erickson would have worked with a dealer to secure vintage wallpaper that was appropriate to the time. "But no one had anything going back that far," he says, "and modern wallpaper just doesn't cut it. It's too hard, too plasticized, and you don't get the soft nap that wallpaper had back then. I could have gone to Scalamandre or another of the big custom designers, but that would have been prohibitively expensive, more than we could afford.

"Fortunately," Erickson continues, "we were in touch with John Burroughs. He's the designer who helped Laura Bush redecorate the Lincoln Bedroom—which used to be Lincoln's office—and he suggested that we check out a place in Richmond called Carter & Company, a mom-and-pop operation that makes historic wallpaper. So I went over there, and what I saw was unbelievable. Their work was just breathtaking, stunning."

"Rick Carter showed them some black-and-white photos of Lincoln's office with the wallpaper in the background," producer Kathleen Kennedy recalls, "and they immediately knew what the colors were and which dyes had been used. Then they reproduced the wallpaper for us using the same hand-screening process used in the nineteenth century—and they were right there in Richmond."

The Past as Present

IN Jack Finney's science fiction novel *Time and Again*, the protagonist travels back in time using not a machine but his imagination. This is possible, Finney suggests, because all eras exist simultaneously. What keeps us in our era is the accumulation of period detail that tells us what year this is—from the models of the cars in the street to the lighting technology in our homes to the coins in our pockets. If we could only loose ourselves from these tethers and persuade our minds that the year was, say, 1865, nothing else would prevent us from visiting other eras.

Finney induces this feat in *Time and Again* by hypnotizing his protagonist and placing him on an elaborately detailed stage set. The set decoration stimulates his imagination; and once he comes to believe that he is living in 1881, he actually is. This is essentially what happened to the actors on the set of *Lincoln*.

"The challenge in a movie like this, when you're trying to achieve a sense of being taken back in time, is never to be distracted by something that feels out of place," producer Kathleen Kennedy says. "What you experience needs to be very consistent in its realization, and that's what I'm most proud of with this movie. I remember seeing the film for the first time and saying to Steven [Spielberg] that what was so extraordinary was that I lost myself and I began to feel as though I were actually witnessing history, as though I were actually traveling back in time."

For such an effort to succeed, two conditions have to be met: the sets have to be incredibly well detailed, and access to them has to be controlled so that the actors' concentration can be protected. "I needed to find locations where Steven and his actors could work in almost a back lot setting, where we had total control of the situation," production designer Rick Carter says. "The warehouse in which we built our interior sets was perfect because it was a controlled area where the actors, especially the president, never had to confront the real world or go out of character."

The culmination of this work was the re-creation of the president's office. "Between takes, I would just walk around and pick up pieces of paper and read them," remembers Joseph Cross, who plays Lincoln secretary John Hay. "They were all real letters that had been sent to Lincoln by people with grievances or questions or requests. Every single detail was accounted for as far as I could see. The work was almost done for you, and you could just play pretend in this world that had been created. You could just exist in it."

To heighten the authenticity, set decorator Jim Erickson researched every possible detail, even which books to put on the shelves. "I contacted the Lincoln Presidential Library in Springfield and asked them what he would have been reading at the time. They gave me a list, and I managed to find about three-quarters of the books in the proper editions."

Erickson made this effort not for theatrical audiences, which won't be able to read the titles on the spines, but for

Set decorator Jim Erickson purchased numerous objects, many of them from the nineteenth century, in order to help create an atmosphere of authenticity on the set.

President Lincoln (Daniel Day-Lewis) working at his object-strewn desk.

the cast. "Rick and I saw the way Daniel [Day-Lewis] was working, and how honestly and perfectly he approached his role, and that challenged us to be as honest and perfect as we could be," Erickson says. "He was consumed by Lincoln for whatever period of time it was, six or eight months, and we wanted to help him by giving him an environment that he could work with."

"You couldn't help but be transported," declares Gloria Reuben, who plays seamstress Elizabeth Keckley. "Walking down that hallway was the most extraordinary experience of my entire career. I loved going to the props department and finding some authentic needles and thread and going back to the set and just sitting there sewing when nobody else was around.

"People often ask me whether actors remain in character all the time on the set," Reuben continues. "All I can say is that if you're an open, creative person and you walk down that hallway, you'll find yourself back in that time."

"People who see movies don't really understand how much excellence goes into the sound, the costumes, the music, the photography," says Sally Field, who portrays Mary Todd Lincoln. "The people who do that work are absolute artists. Ben Burtt, the sound designer, could have recorded any mantelpiece clock he wanted, but he went to the trouble of finding Lincoln's actual mantelpiece clock because that's his artistry. It didn't matter to him whether anyone else knew it was Lincoln's clock. He knew, and that's the difference between someone who's good and someone who's great."

JANUSZ Kaminski, *Lincoln*'s director of photography, thinks of himself as a "visual storyteller." It's his job, he says, to take the words of the written script and translate them into the visual language of film. "What I do is nonverbal," he explains. "I work with light and shadow and camera angles to create a visual language that supports the story being told."

Like all languages, the dialects of cinematography have specific grammatical rules. For the most part, these rules are followed, but sometimes they're broken intentionally to create a particular effect or suit a particular purpose. In historical films such as *Lincoln*, the lighting rules often relate to the technology of the period. In 1865, for example, the most common sources of illumination were the sun during the day and candlelight and gaslight at night. To the extent that he could, Kaminski made use of these naturalistic light sources. "But it would have been impossible to light a film directed by Steven Spielberg using just sunlight, gaslight, and candlelight. A different kind of movie maybe you could have shot with only natural light and high-speed digital cameras, but not a Steven Spielberg movie."

Kaminski's central rule was that the light in a scene should always be attributable to a light source visible within the frame. "I followed that rule, but I also took liberties," Kaminski says. "I'd have candlelight in a scene, but if I tried to light the scene entirely with candlelight, the audience wouldn't be able to see anything, because there wouldn't be enough light. So I supplemented the candlelight with artificial movie lights. But I did this in such a way that I created the illusion of a room lit only by candlelight."

Following the "within the frame" rule, Kaminski staged most of the interior daytime scenes near windows so that the artificial light would appear to be sunlight streaming in from outside. For nighttime scenes, the light source had to be accounted for in more creative ways. "If a torch made sense, we'd use a torch, or maybe a gas lamp or a fireplace," Kaminski says. "Even in a nonelectric era, there are still plenty of light sources you can work with."

OPPOSITE: **The set for the War Department telegraph office.**

Illuminating a Bygone Era

"Part of my job is to create a sense of reality," he continues, "but I also have a responsibility to tell the story in a dramatic way. Sometimes the logic of the lighting conflicts with the logic of the drama, and I have to create off-screen light that serves my dramatic purpose while still seeming naturalistic."

Kaminski also serves his dramatic purpose by manipulating light and shadow, especially on the faces of the actors. "During the 1930s and 1940s, cinematographers would light characters according to what they represented in the story," he explains. "They would create shadows on the faces of bad characters to make them look sinister and light good characters brightly to make them seem virtuous. But we don't do that anymore because the actors are so good now and audiences are more sophisticated. Instead, we generally let the audience discover the characters through the story and the performances. But it can be interesting sometimes to go the opposite direction.

"*Schindler's List* is a good example," continues Kaminski, who directed the photography for that Spielberg film as well. "The concentration camp commander, Amon Goeth—I lit him always with a beautiful, almost angelic light because, in my opinion, there was no ambiguity to his character. Schindler, on the other hand, I frequently lit with shadows and half-light because there was a struggle going on inside him, and he wasn't sure who he was. Am I good? Am I learning to be good? What is my role in this story? What should I be doing? Only at the end, when these questions are resolved, do I light him brightly, without any shadows, to show that he has found himself."

In *Lincoln*, the president suffers from a similar self-doubt concerning his handling of the war. So Kaminski employed a similar strategy, using shadow to emphasize the deep set of Daniel Day-Lewis' eyes and the age lines that makeup designer Lois Burwell applied to his face. Near the end of the film, however, Kaminski brightens the light as the president succeeds in persuading reluctant congressmen to vote his way on abolition. "He moves into the light, and the brightness eliminates the shadows from his eyes," Kaminski says. "Now you look into those eyes and see Lincoln's confidence that his vision will prevail."

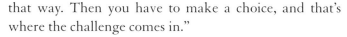

Leaps of Faith

LET'S be clear from the start: within the context of serious historical filmmaking, taking dramatic license doesn't mean radically altering facts to suit the needs of a particular viewpoint or story line. There are certainly instances in which filmmakers balance the competing dictates of story and history, but these don't include reversing the results of an election or making Napoleon the winner at Waterloo. Far more often, dramatic license comes into play when facts aren't known, either because the information has been lost or because it was never written down in the first place. When that happens, or when the historical record is otherwise unclear, filmmakers have no choice but to fill in the gaps with their own good judgment and imaginations as best they can.

"Every person in every department worked very, very hard to make this film as authentic as possible," producer Kathleen Kennedy says. "The challenge was that sometimes you just didn't know what really happened. It could have been this way, or it could have been

that way. Then you have to make a choice, and that's where the challenge comes in."

On the other hand, lack of knowledge can sometimes create an opportunity. "The hair and makeup and wardrobe people came to my house in Los Angeles months before the shoot with all these samples and drawings and pictures," recalls James Spader, who plays lobbyist William N. Bilbo. "I remember they had this book with them. It had archival photos of nearly every key character in the film except mine. They had done fairly extensive research but hadn't been able to find a single image of Bilbo. 'Great, that's fine,' I said, because having no image meant we could take some liberties.

"We had no idea whether the real Bilbo had a mustache or not, but this Bilbo has a big bushy mustache," Spader continues. "We didn't know whether the real Bilbo was well groomed or not, but this Bilbo isn't. His hair has a life of its own. We didn't know whether the real Bilbo was a heavy drinker, but I asked the makeup department to paint tiny broken blood vessels on my face so that this Bilbo could be a man who had led a life that was lustful and grand, because that served the story we were telling. There was nothing in the research I did and [screenwriter] Tony Kushner did that definitively supported this interpretation, but there wasn't anything in the research that contradicted it, either, and so we went with it."

Production designer Rick Carter calls these choices "aesthetic leaps of faith" because, although informed

William N. Bilbo (James Spader) confers with Secretary of State William H. Seward (David Strathairn) on delicate matters of political persuasion.

A congressman responds succinctly to Bilbo's efforts to obtain his vote for the Thirteenth Amendment.

by historical research, they remain essentially judgment calls. "In designing a movie, you try to become aesthetically linked in your mind to the story you're trying to tell and the subject as it exists in history," Carter says. "Somewhere in between, you develop an interpretation that's true both to the story and to the history."

A case in point is the color scheme Carter used for the White House interiors. Period photographs, being monochrome, don't reveal the true colors of the paint and wallpaper, so Carter had to rely on other sources to create a close-enough palette from which to work. Then he made choices, not all of which were based exclusively on historical accuracy. "People used a lot of garish colors back then, so we made the sets colorful but only up to a point," Carter says. "The basic tone of the film was quite serious, and we didn't want gaudiness to get in the way of the drama.

"Every choice you make in a situation like that is tied to historical facts," Carter continues, "but not everything can be exactly as it was. We're not making a movie there,

in 1865—we're making a movie here, today—and that means our interpretation will be a little different."

The purpose of making a historical film, after all, isn't simply to reproduce the past. Rather, it's to tell a meaningful story by interpreting the past; and every storyteller is entitled to his own interpretation.

WE knew from brief mentions of Bilbo in letters and diaries that he was considered a sharp dresser and a bit of a dandy. But we didn't know much else, and that gave me the opening to play him as a rogue—completely unreserved, bombastic, somewhat larger than life—which served the drama much better than a reserved Bilbo would have.

—JAMES SPADER

A Score Short and Quiet

"A LISTENER'S response to music is greatly informed by his acculturation," composer John Williams says. "If a person is unfamiliar with a particular harmonic or melodic idiom—say, an idiom from another continent—its visceral or corporal effect might differ greatly from its effect on someone from a different culture. Mozart's Prague Symphony, as an example, might not have the same meaning to listeners in Tibet as it might to listeners in a European audience.

"Responses to music also change over time," Williams continues. "The same piece of music might evoke a very different reaction in you than it might in your grandmother, due to generational differences in thoughts, memories, and experiences. The same can be said of audiovisual experiences like watching a film. We can watch *Lincoln* in ten or twenty years' time, and the experience would be very different from the one we would have watching it today."

When John Williams begins to compose a score, he brings his own acculturation to the process. He watches a film again and again to assess its needs, and then begins to write. "I'm directed by a largely intuitive process," he says. "Steven [Spielberg] and I talk, but not in the kind of words that you and I would exchange. Our discussions take place over the piano. I'll play fragments for him— musical ideas—and we'll discuss their effect."

Initially, Williams considered developing a single musical theme for *Lincoln*, perhaps based on a nineteenth-century tune that Lincoln himself might have recognized. But as Williams studied the film, he discovered that no single theme, or even two, would be sufficient. "The dramatic and atmospheric needs of the film required very separate pieces that I realized I'd have to compose anew," Williams recalls. "What was unusual about this score was that I rarely used the same theme twice. It required the creation of quite a breadth of material, despite being a relatively short and quiet score."

Williams developed a number of principal themes for *Lincoln*—all of which draw, to a greater or lesser degree, on his deep familiarity with the nineteenth-century American musical vernacular. "With Malice Toward None" was created to accompany speeches being made by President Lincoln. "It's in the character of a Protestant hymn," Williams explains, "but without any overt sense of religiosity. Its purpose is to provide a reverential background for Lincoln's words."

"The People's House" was composed for scenes that take place in the U.S. Congress, particularly the scene near the end of the film, in which freedpeople enter the

ABOVE: **Sheet music for a few of the patriotic songs that became popular during the Civil War.**

House of Representatives to witness the vote on the Thirteenth Amendment. "It's a more anthemic piece," Williams says, "quite different from 'With Malice Toward None' and less steeped in the musical vocabulary of the nineteenth century."

"The Blue and Grey" is essentially a lament, which underscores the scene in which Lincoln witnesses the devastation and incomprehensible loss suffered on the battlefield at Petersburg, Virginia.

In creating these themes, Williams took into account not only his own acculturation but also that of his audience. "I don't make a deliberate attempt to tap into a collective memory," Williams says, "but it does happen. The audience's physiological and emotional response to music is something that I still can't explain, even after sixty-five years of composing. I don't think any-one can. It's one of the miraculous things about music that connects people in profound and unexpected ways."

FOR a number of years, I've periodically conducted the Chicago Symphony. The orchestra is universally recognized as one of the best in the world, and every time I returned from Chicago, I said to Steven, "Someday we should do something with this orchestra," never really thinking that it would be practical. As we approached the time to make decisions about where, when, and how to do the music for *Lincoln*, Steven said, "You know, wouldn't it be a great time to have your friends at the Chicago Symphony perform on the soundtrack?" So we recorded the score at Symphony Hall in Chicago. The quality of the playing is personal and of very high artistic standard. It was particularly inspiring to note that Illinois was the first state to ratify the Thirteenth Amendment. I thought that made a very real spiritual connection.

—JOHN WILLIAMS

President Lincoln (Daniel Day-Lewis) delivering his second inaugural address.

The Past's Sonic Fabric

"IN the false world of the movie set, there is very little valid sound," Ben Burtt explains. "Actors walk on floors made of plywood—not, say, the metal of a spaceship—so the sound of their footsteps is all wrong."

It's the job of sound designers such as Burtt to make sure those footsteps sound plausible, but his responsibilities don't end there. More generally, sound designers manipulate what audiences hear in order to enhance their experience of the film. Like the composer of the score, the sound designer helps the director tell the film's story by underscoring the action and amplifying the emotions it evokes. Because the sounds necessary to accomplish this aren't available in the artificial environment of the set, sound designers have to look elsewhere for the sounds they need.

Lincoln posed several unique challenges for Burtt, who is best known for his Academy Award–winning work on the original *Star Wars* and *E.T.: The Extra-Terrestrial.* "In my career," he says, "I've worked on films that have given me a great deal of freedom from reality. I haven't had to work much with everyday situations. Instead, I've been able to design sounds from a very customized point of view."

Working outside reality has led Burtt to rely heavily on unusual field recordings and the use of customized props and synthesizers. Some of his work is straightforward. To create the sound of footsteps in a spaceship, for instance, Burtt simply employs a Foley artist to record the sound of someone walking across a sheet of metal. (Foley artists record particular sound effects, such as footsteps and the handling of props, in a recording studio while watching playbacks of film footage.) Other sounds, such as the "voice" of the *Star Wars* android R2-D2, require a great deal more complexity and creativity but are likewise artificially created.

These techniques and Burtt's extensive library could have supplied all of the sounds needed for *Lincoln*, but

Burtt had a more ambitious plan in mind: he wanted to research and record historic sounds that would have been familiar to residents of Washington in 1865. "We could have easily gone down the path of recording sounds close at hand," Burtt acknowledges. "If I needed the sound of a clock ticking, I could have recorded any antique clock, even a period clock I have in my own home. But I had this other idea: why not search out sounds that Lincoln might actually have heard?

"Most of the time in movies, we don't approach sound so literally," Burtt continues. "When I'm working on a Star Trek movie, I don't think a lot about what kind of shoes Captain Kirk is wearing, I'm thinking more about trying to invent imaginary sounds that will work emotionally in the context of the story. But with a historical film like *Lincoln*, everyone is trying to be as authentic as possible, so I had to think more literally."

Given that sound recording wasn't invented until 1877, Burtt couldn't use archival recordings. But he was able to unearth authentic artifacts that make essentially the same sounds today as they made in 1865. Through his research, for example, Burtt learned that the Studebaker National Museum in South Bend, Indiana, had in its collection the carriage that transported Lincoln to Ford's Theatre on the night of his assassination. "I contacted the museum and asked if we could record some of the sounds associated with the carriage," Burtt recalls. "Of course, we couldn't take it out on the road and pull it with horses, but we did hire a local soundman, who recorded the sound of the doors opening and closing. He also pushed

OPPOSITE: **During his research, Ben Burtt learned that the pocket watch believed to have been carried by President Lincoln on the night of his assassination had been donated by the descendants of Robert Todd Lincoln to the Kentucky Historical Society. With the cooperation of the society, Burtt arranged for the ticking of that watch to be recorded using a special soundproof box.**

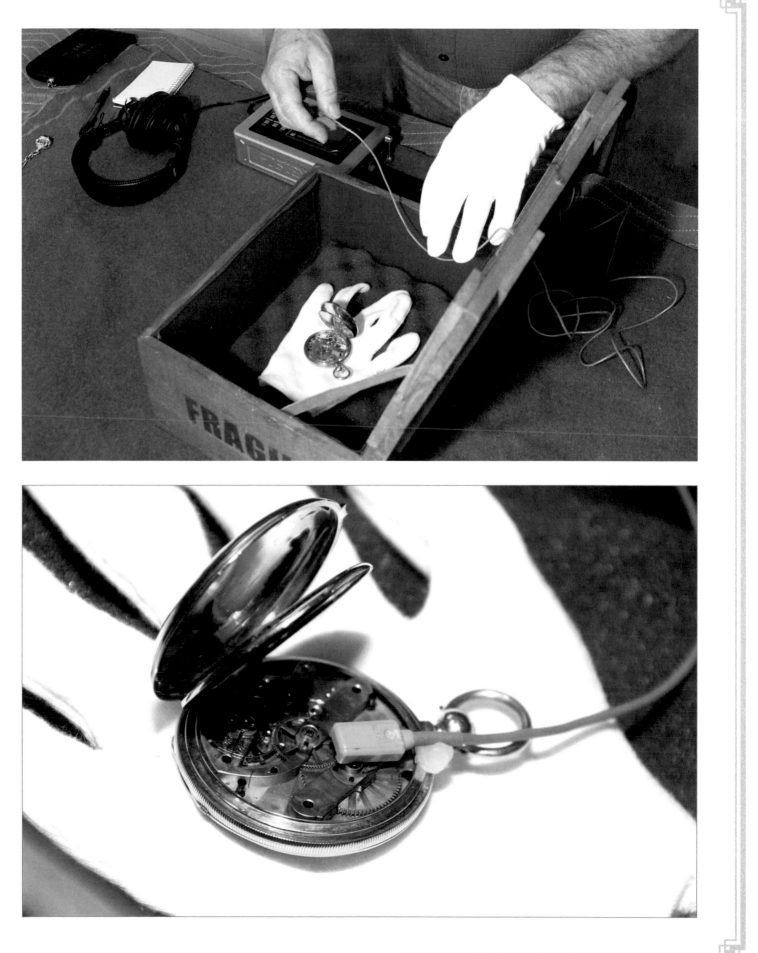

Preston Blair (Hal Holbrook) with the president (Daniel Day-Lewis) in his White House office.

down on the seat and recorded the sound of the springs squeaking. We used those sounds many times in the film during the carriage scenes."

On one of his own research trips, Burtt personally visited the White House to make a recording of the French portico clock that sat on the mantel in President Lincoln's second-floor office. The ticking of that clock is a sound Lincoln heard nearly every day of his presidency; and it's still in the White House, ticking away. "I went there with a partner, Greg Smith, because I wanted to have a second set of equipment as a backup," Burtt remembers. "We recorded the portico clock and two other French clocks, all of which were purchased during Andrew Jackson's administration and were still being used in Lincoln's time. They're little clocks with short pendulums, so they tick rather fast—not the slow *tick . . . tock . . . tick . . . tock* of a grandfather clock, but the rapid *plink-plink-plink* of a metronome."

Because the ticking of the portico clock is subtle and difficult to hear, especially over the bustle of the White House, Burtt used a special contact microphone that works on the same principle as a medical stethoscope. It attaches to an object and thus picks up the sound vibrations directly, minimizing ambient noise. In this way, Burtt was able to obtain clean, crisp recordings of the clock, but they weren't ready yet for use in the film. "The contact mike provides such a close-up perspective that you hear every little turn of the mechanism—it's like putting your ear up to the casing," he says. "So I did something that we call worldizing. I took the original recording and I made a ten-minute loop. Then I set up a little sound system in an empty historic house here in California—it happened to be up for sale at the time, so there was nobody around—and I placed microphones around the room and out in the hallway. Finally, I played the loop on the sound system and made new stereo recordings of the sound of the portico clock from several different acoustic perspectives. Those are the recordings we used in the film."

Worldizing is especially important when sounds have been recorded in different acoustic spaces. For example, if dialogue has been recorded in a tiled bathroom, sound effects recorded in a studio will sound odd unless they are worldized. "If you heard the original contact-mike recording of the portico clock, it would sound strange to you, because people don't listen to clocks with their ears pressed to the casing," Burtt continues. "Even though the ticking is completely authentic, the acoustic space isn't. Worldizing places the sound in the right acoustic space for a particular scene."

Much of Burtt's other work on *Lincoln* was similarly subtle and detail oriented. "Normally, I could tell you that we created the sound for the big truck chase out of lion roars to make the trucks seem especially animalistic, but I can't give any examples like that for *Lincoln*," he says. "For this film, I went to a great deal of effort to record fireplace crackle—the sound of logs burning in a fireplace. I recorded fires in my own house and in other people's houses—I created an entire library of fireplace crackle—because so many scenes in *Lincoln* take place in rooms with working fireplaces, and I wanted to have just the right little crackle fall between the lines of dialogue. It's not something that will make you stop in the theater and say, 'Oh, what great crackle,' but it puts you in the room and gives you a nice sense of coziness."

Other small touches include the use of an off-screen train whistle, which required Burtt first to research period trains and then locate one with an appropriate whistle. "A sound like that tells you there's other activity in the world beyond the action in the scene," Burtt says. "We want to remind the audience that there are other people outside the room and even across town who are doing things at the same time that matter just as much to them. *Lincoln* is filled with lots of little subtleties like that. The point is to expand the horizon of the movie."

HISTORIC sound is a fleeting sort of thing. Unless someone saves a sound by recording it, there's no way to get the sound back once it has gone. Maybe in the future someone will invent a technology to retrieve audio from the past. I don't know what that would be, but maybe ancient Greek vases will turn out to have grooves, created by vibrations, that someone will figure out how to play.

—BEN BURTT

One of the most important scenes in the film, at least from Ben Burtt's perspective, takes place in the president's office as Lincoln awaits news of the House vote on the Thirteenth Amendment. Just as the production team went to great effort to re-create the physical space of Lincoln's office, so did Burtt take pains to re-create its acoustic space, beginning with the ticking of the portico clock. "For a few moments, nobody talks, there's no music, and all you hear is the ticking of the clock. That tells you how quiet the room is, because it gives you something to measure against. If you can hear the ticking of the clock, it tells you there isn't any other sound in the room, and it sets a tone."

The sound of an off-screen cannonade finally interrupts the ticking, indicating that the House has passed the amendment. Although the cannonade wasn't in the original script, Burtt discovered in his research that the news of the vote was spread in this way, so he included it in the soundtrack, recording the necessary sounds during a live-ammunition demonstration of period cannon at the Bull Run battlefield. "You hear the ticking of the clock, and suddenly you hear this *boom boom boom*, and it catches the president's attention," Burtt explains. "So he goes over to the window and slides it open, and he hears not only the booming of the guns but also the ringing of a church bell—the sound of freedom ringing."

Burtt didn't use just any church bell, of course. While in Washington, he recorded the bell at the historic St. John's Episcopal Church, located just across Lafayette Square from the White House. It was cast by Paul Revere's son in 1822 and still hangs in the church's steeple. Thus, Burtt recorded the same bell President Lincoln would have heard on January 31, 1865. "This section of the movie is just thirty seconds long," Burtt says, "but it's a thoroughly reconstructed moment, built out of the actual sonic fabric of the past, and it really delivers something powerful to the audience."

AFTERWORD

❖ ❖ ❖

TONY KUSHNER

I T'S COUNTERINTUITIVE (or, as Abraham Lincoln might have put it, ass-backward) to ask the screenwriter to provide the ending rather than the beginning for a book about the making of a film. Screenwriters are the alpha rather than the omega, the inception rather than the conclusion, the conception rather than. . . . Well, you get the idea. The egg rather than the chicken. If we were adhering to the order in which things happen in filmmaking, I should have written the preface, or the first chapter.

I was present throughout the making of the film, and I have many stories to tell about what I saw on the set, what I admired, what I gleaned, what was struggled over, struggled against, the exhilarating heights, the slough of despond, the anxiety-overeating at the craft services table. Most of these stories are far livelier than anything I have to relate about the writing of the script. Who wants to read about what it's like to write? I'd rather tell you the story about the day we were filming in Petersburg, Virginia, when I nearly ran into Daniel Day-Lewis moments before he was about to start shooting a difficult scene; not wanting to distract him, I ducked out of sight behind one of the extras playing a soldier. The soldier, startled, started to turn around. "Don't turn around! Face forward!" I hissed. "What are you hiding from?" he asked over his shoulder. I replied "The President!" "Why?" he asked, "What did you do?" I snapped back, "I wrote the script!"

In February 2006, after we'd finished making *Munich*, Steven Spielberg asked me to consider writing the screenplay for a film about Abraham Lincoln. I told him I'd consider it, while thinking to myself "Abraham Lincoln!" and also "I've got to find a nice way to say no."

On April 25, 2006, Steven and Kathy Kennedy invited me to join them and a group of fifteen leading Lincoln historians for a six-hour long, free-ranging discussion regarding the sixteenth president. Afterward, Steven and I talked. He promised I wouldn't have to write big battle scenes, since he didn't want to film them, and, agreeing that it would be a mistake to attempt to cover all four years of Lincoln's presidency, he approved the idea of focusing on a meaningful portion of it.

I called my father in Louisiana. He greatly admired Lincoln and told me he hoped I'd say yes. I realized that I wanted to say yes. So I did.

Here's how the making of *Lincoln*, at least my part of it, really began. I met with Steven a few days after telling him I'd write the script, and on the first page of my first *Lincoln* notebook he made a drawing. According to the notes I scrawled around Steven's drawing, the figure on the right, "L at Soldiers' Home in rocker," is Lincoln, in his summer residence, sitting in a rocking chair, staring out the window. Behind him are "the rivals at the White House," meaning Lincoln's rivals—Seward, Chase, and Bates—seated around the cabinet table. In the illegible scribble on the right, I wrote "Shifts in time & place when it's Lincoln's POV." At that meeting, Steven and I discussed treating time and place in the film fluidly, expressively, rather than realistically and consecutively—I suppose as a means of attempting to approximate Lincoln's empathic, athletic, unbounded, and boundaryless imagination.

Eventually, the sheer narrative force of Lincoln's life, sufficient in its dramatic perfection to make even agnostics and disbelievers pause to wonder about the role of Providence in politics, won out. Without discussing it, we gravitated toward Lincoln in the objective context of his place and time, and largely abandoned the impulse to contextualize the world within Lincoln's subjectivity. He may have made the world resemble what he dreamed it ought to be, but he knew the world was not his dream.

Lincoln blazes from his historical time to the present, an inextinguishable, glorious light. Ralph Waldo Emerson declared, in his funeral oration, that Lincoln's "occupying the chair of State was a triumph of the good sense of mankind," and no serious person would argue with him. Secretary of War Edwin Stanton, in his eulogy at the private funeral service in the White House, said that Lincoln was a

figure of superlative discipline, "the most powerful ruler of men the world has ever seen . . . [b]ecause he was the most perfect ruler of himself," which is also inarguable. Lincoln's accomplishment is comprehensible now, in hindsight, in all its supreme, overarching rationality.

I believe that Lincoln the lawyer, the lawgiver, the reasonable and accessible man of the people is the Lincoln that originally appealed to Steven as a personality worthy of admiration, and as a subject worthy of a film. Steven, it seems to me, is a filmmaker for whom narrative is shaped and guided by a deeply democratic ethic. But as Herman Melville knew, and as Spielberg knows, there's darkness shadowing democracy, there's sacrifice and strangeness and mystery. This is expressed nowhere more beautifully or powerfully than in the life of Abraham Lincoln, in which thought and action, empathy and ruthlessness, progress and tragedy were set in dialectical spin in both the fathomless caverns of the interior and on the world's stage. From the beginning of the making of this film, Steven has been attracted to the complexity of Lincoln's spirit as well as to its accessibility, to the darkness of Lincoln as well as to his light.

After he made the drawing in my notebook, Steven talked about how taken he'd been by accounts of the gloominess of the White House, especially at night, when the oil lamps and gas jets had to be snuffed for fear of fire. When Lincoln took the solitary, nocturnal walks for which he became famous, "it must have been," Steven told me, "like he was walking through a haunted house."

I shared Steven's divided loyalty between Lincoln's light and his darkness. Daniel Day-Lewis incarnated it. Almost everyone who's spent time with Lincoln concludes, as Carl Sandburg did after his epic effort to encompass the man, that in order to truly describe Lincoln, you must "put in mystery without end. Then add mystery."

I think that what I'm proudest of in *Lincoln*—apart from the fact that we did it, we made it, the first studio film about Abraham Lincoln in seventy-two years— and what I hope people will find in it, is an exploration of the rational processes of a people's government that observes and honors its mysteries, both sorrowful and glorious—or as Lincoln would say, for weal or for woe.

At Steven and Kathy's conference of Lincoln historians in April 2006, I met Doris Kearns Goodwin for the first time. We spoke after the other historians had gone. Doris sympathized with the fear of failure that was making me hesitate, but she told me that, whether or not I was successful, I would never regret any time I spent with Abraham Lincoln.

Many people made *Lincoln*, and of course I can't speak for all of them, but now that it's over, now that it's done, I suspect no one involved would disagree with me: Doris was right. ✌☉

ACKNOWLEDGMENTS

The publisher and producers would like to thank the following for their extraordinary support and contributions to this project:

Steven Spielberg, Kathleen Kennedy, and Tony Kushner

Ben Burtt, Lois Burwell, Rick Carter, Jim Erickson, Sally Field, Joanna Johnston, Hal Holbrook, Janusz Kaminski, Gloria Reuben, James Spader, and John Williams

Kristie Macosko Krieger, Samantha Becker, John Swartz, Marvin Levy, and Kristin Stark

Steve Newman, Theresa Cross, and Kevin Campbell

Laurent Bouzereau

David Rubel would like to thank James M. McPherson and Eric Foner for teaching him all the best things he knows about the Civil War and Reconstruction.

For information address Disney Editions,
1133 Avenue of the Americas, New York, NY 10036

Produced by Welcome Enterprises, Inc.
6 West 18th Street, New York, NY 10011
www.welcomebooks.com
Project Director & Book Designer: H. Clark Wakabayashi

Coproduced by Agincourt Press
President: David Rubel
Senior Editor/Photo Research: Julia Rubel
Interview Transcriptions: Abigail Rubel

Movie photography by David James
Illustrations on pages 4–5, 14–15, 52–53, 140–141, and 176–177 by James Clyne
Costume sketches on pages 188, 191, and 193 by Richard Merritt

ISBN 978-1-4231-8199-6
F322-8368-0-13060
Printed in the United States of America
FIRST EDITION
10 9 8 7 6 5 4 3 2

Now he belongs to the ages.

—EDWIN M. STANTON

Portrait of Abraham Lincoln taken by Alexander Gardner
four days before the president was shot by John Wilkes Booth
at Ford's Theatre in Washington, D.C., on April 14, 1865.